Sex Discrimination in Educational Employment

Legal Strategies and Alternatives

Cynthia Stoddard
with
Antoinette Little

Learning Publications, Inc.
Holmes Beach, Fla.

Learning Publications Series in
Women in Education

Co-Editors:
Judith Brawer
Edsel Erickson

Library of Congress Number: 80-82019

Learning Publications, Inc.
P.O. Box 1326
Holmes Beach, Florida 33509

Hardcover ISBN 0-918452-26-0
Softcover ISBN 0-918452-27-9

Cover Design by Rob Gutek

Printing   1   2   3   4   5   6   7   8
Year   1   2   3   4   5

Printed in the United States of America

To my parents, Gordon and Mary Stoodard, who made a contribution beyond measuring—their love.

Acknowledgements

There are many, many people who contributed to this project in a variety of ways, but a few warrant special recognition.

First and foremost, my husband, Robert A. Novosad, who is deserving of an award for his understanding and never-ending support and encouragement, not only in this project, but in all I have ever undertaken.

Judith Brawer, the editor of this book, who gave new meaning to the word "patience,"

Edsel Erickson, who made this entire project possible by his belief in the need to educate educators on their basic employment rights.

Finally, Janet Haynes, Patricia Wyckoff and Kay Babcock, who served as sounding boards more often than they probably realize and who cared enough to listen when I needed an audience.

PREFACE

This book is intended to inform employers, their employees charged with equal employment responsibilities, and female employees within the educational field, of the laws, procedures, remedies and issues relating to state and federal prohibition of sex based terms and conditions of employment.

Employment, under these laws, defines an activity commencing at recruitment and ending at retirement. The various laws regulate not only hours, wages and fringe benefits, and other concrete terms of the various steps in the employment continuum, but the amenities of the work place as well, such as sexual harassment, pre-employment inquiries, and pregnancy related benefits.

This book does not provide a laundry list of all possible violations to be memorized by wary employers or scrutinized by disgruntled employees. Instead, these pages contain a statement of the philosophic basis of civil rights statutes, the elements of a violation, and a summary of court decisions in common fact situations. It concludes by setting out the procedures by which an employee sets enforcement in action.

Neither employer nor employee should expect certainty in this area of the law. One must *understand* not *remember* as these laws do not define prohibited acts but instead generally require equal treatment of males and females. These laws do not prohibit discrimination on work related bases, e.g. necessary educational credentials and experience. These laws do not prohibit unfairness, unreasonableness, low pay, poor working condition or even mayhem UNLESS the adversity falls on only one sex. This body of law deals only with the relative treatment of males and females (and other protected classes).

Court cases decided under these laws have highlighted prohibited behaviors and resulted in amendment to the underlying statute. Specific behavior not prohibited by courts one day may be prohibited the next. No text in this area of law which seeks to comprehensively state "rules" will be valid in six months. This text, therefore seeks to explain the undergirding, the intent, the goals of the various equal employment laws which remain constant.

An employer armed with an understanding of this basic premise will be relieved from the anxiety of violation of copious specific prohibitions. This understanding coupled with commitment to comply, may require scrutiny of past practices and assumptions. New systems set up to deal with each individual on the basis of his/her JOB RELATED QUALIFICATIONS will not run afoul of the law, provided that employer past practices have not, in some manner, prohibited females from acquiring these qualifications.

An employee with the same understanding can accurately assess and explain violations of these laws. These abilities can expedite speedy, in-house resolution of issues where both parties are committed to compliance with the law. They can, as well, measurably increase the likelihood of efficient resolution of the controversy if recourse to outside tribunals becomes necessary.

Compliance with these laws is not costly. To the contrary, compliance assures that the individual best able to perform a function will have the job. The burden of private enforcement of these laws, however, is great on both employers and employees. The costs in out-of-pocket expenditures and time are transferred to the consumer of the employer's product. In the field of education, the consumer that pays is the student.

Clearly the better course is compliance. As the field of education is populated in both employer and employee strata by persons professionally committed to the education of students, only misunderstanding of the law could account for its violation and concommitant burdening students. It is our hope that this text removes these obstacles to full compliance.

Antoinette Little

Kalamazoo, Michigan
January 1981

TABLE OF CONTENTS

Chapter I

INTRODUCTION

The application of sex discrimination laws to educational employment is fairly recent. Title VII of the Civil Rights Act of 1964, which is the primary protection against employment discrimination based on sex, initially excluded school employment. It wasn't until 1972 that Title VII was amended to extend its coverage to people employed in education. This amendment now enables thousands of individuals—teachers, professional staff and nonprofessional staff—in some 120,000 educational institutions to assert certain basic rights in seeking equal employment opportunities.

Because the extension of protection to school employment is so recent, many of those affected do not yet fully understand how the law applies to their own employment situations. In order to better understand their rights, women in school employment need to know exactly what employment rights are guaranteed under the law, what responsibilities the employer has in establishing nondiscriminatory policies, and what means are available to a woman in seeking a remedy for violations of these rights.

The primary intent of Title VII is to provide equal opportunity in employment to ALL individuals regardless of race, color, religion, sex, or national origin. The purpose of this book is to help women employed in the educational field to better understand how this law applies to them.

In order to effectively assert a right guaranteed by law, an individual must know what is included in that right as well as any limitations on it, and what constitutes a violation of that right. However, reading legal documents can sometimes be confusing to people who are unfamiliar with the law and its specialized vocabulary, and there is very little literature currently available to help the laywoman understand her employment rights.

This book explains in clear, nontechnical language, what sex discrimination in employment is, explores the various laws which might be involved, discusses some specific issues in educational employment where the right to equal employment opportunity is protected, and describes the remedies that are available.

Knowing what rights are protected under the law is not the end of the problem. A woman also has to know how to go about asserting her rights and getting relief for the wrongs suffered. The elements of what it takes to prove a charge of sex discrimination are examined in this book and the legal procedures are clearly described.

Procedure is all important in the area of sex discrimination; it can make or break a valid claim. Because procedure is so very important in claiming a violation of Title VII, the final chapter has been devoted to procedural requirements for filing a complaint, where to file a complaint, how to file, and when to file.

Knowing what your rights are is important, but acting when those rights are violated is even more important. No one is likely to assert your rights for you—it is a highly personal area—and if a woman truly wants to improve what she believes to be discriminatory work conditions, she is probably going to have to use Title VII to assert her rights.

Deciding to file a sex discrimination complaint is not always an easy decision to make. All of the pros and cons have to be considered. The obvious desired result is an improvement in the working conditions, increased employment opportunities, and equal pay. However, this has to be weighed against the time, expense, inconvenience, and negative responses of co-workers and employer when filing a Title VII complaint. Before any complaint is filed, a woman should be sure that she is ready to handle all of this—including the adverse attitudes and perhaps even ridicule she may be subjected to.

Although some of the effects of filing a sex discrimination complaint can be unpleasant, more and more women are coming to realize that any unpleasantness may be far outweighed by the relief they ultimately receive. The relief available under Title VII is very comprehensive. For every wrong there is a specific relief to which an employee may be entitled.

In drafting Title VII, Congress was well aware of the fact that many employees might be dissuaded by employers from filing complaints. To encourage employees to assert their rights, specific provisions were included in Title VII which prohibit any reprisal or retaliation by an employer against an employee who files a complaint under Title VII.

This book does not attempt to be a final or comprehensive analysis of the law as it exists today. The areas of civil rights and equal employment opportunities are new and extremely volatile ones. Court decisions are constantly being handed down which shape and modify the statutory language of Title VII. Because of this constant state of flux, a woman who wishes to file a complaint should always consult with an attorney, or an Equal Employment Opportunity agency representative, to be sure that the law, as she understands it, is still being interpreted or upheld in accordance with her understanding.

An example of this is in the regulations protecting the rights of pregnant working women. Prior to 1979, the United States Supreme Court on two occasions held that pregnancy and pregnancy-related problems were not distinctions based on gender when an employer denied equal opportunity to pregnant employees. The Court indicated that Congressional intent to protect pregnant workers as a specific group was not apparent in the language of Title VII. Congress reacted to these decisions by the passage of the Pregnancy Discrimination Act of 1979. The Act now provides specific protection for pregnant workers. In this example, the Congress reacted to a court decision which shaped the interpretation of Title VII, and passed legislation which drastically changed the rights and responsibilities of employees and employers.

It cannot be emphasized enough that this book serves only as an introduction to the area of fair employment practices. It is not meant to be a substitute for seeking legal advice. While it is possible for an individual to file her complaint without an attorney, the complexities of the case and procedural requirements may make it advisable to retain an attorney.

The idea for this book arose from a desire to help women better understand their employment rights. This desire to instruct is the underlying theme of the book. The manual is not a "fire and brimstone" approach to the employment inequities of women as a whole. Rather, it is a logical and simple approach to the laws and their application to women in an individual way.

It is hoped that, through this book, women will learn what their various employment rights are, and when confronted with a discriminatory situation, that they will use this new-found knowledge to assert a valid claim of sex discrimination.

The primary objective in writing this book has been to explain the laws in such a way that a woman will be able to make an informed assessment of her employment situation, will investigate what her rights are, know what questions to ask if she is uncertain in any area, and most important, will know how to proceed in asserting her rights.

A secondary objective was to reduce the complexity of the laws to a point where they seemed less obscure and formidable—to make the laws appear as a helpful tool, rather than a maze of words designed to trip up the uninformed. Hopefully, this will reduce the frustration experienced by many as they attempt to find their way through legal intricacies and unfamiliar language to an understanding of the law and its application.

Chapter II
OVERVIEW OF
EQUAL EMPLOYMENT LAWS

Title VII

Title VII of the Civil Rights Act is the primary law used by women in asserting their employment rights. Title VII prohibits discrimination on the basis of race, color, religion, sex or national origin in all employment practices and policies, including hiring, firing, promotion, compensation and other terms, privileges and conditions of employment. The 1972 Amendments extend the law's protection to women in educational employment. The Equal Employment Opportunity Commission (EEOC) was created to administer Title VII and to assure equal treatment for all in employment.

As amended, Title VII establishes that any employer with 15 or more employees will be subject to sanctions for any unlawful employment practices. The 15 employees can be full-time or part-time, faculty, staff, or administrators, employed in any department; the figure represents a cumulative count, not a department by department or school by school number. If a school has only 13 employees, but it is part of a school system having more than 15 employees, that school will be subject to Title VII sanctions.

Since the passage of the Civil Rights Act in 1964, many cases have been decided, guidelines and regulations have been issued, and formal amendments have been made, to shape and define the rights of working women. Some of the major issues covered by Title VII, such as compensation and fringe benefits, are covered in detail in the next chapter.

Title VII sets out what acts constitute unlawful discrimination on the basis of sex in the employment context. The provisions of the law are wide-ranging and comprehensive in the protection afforded to women in the workforce. It is defined as unlawful discrimination to fail or refuse to hire or to discharge any individual, or otherwise to discriminate against any individual with respect to his compensation terms, conditions, or privileges of employment; or to limit, segregate, or classify employees or applicants for employment in any way which would deprive or tend to deprive any individual of employment opportunities or adversely effect the status as an employee because of sex. The law applies to applicants for employment as well as employees.

As defined, an unlawful employment practice is any practice on the part of the employer which is motivated, premised or conditioned upon the sex of an employee, or any seemingly neutral practice which has an adverse impact on one sex. For women, this serves to guarantee their ability to strive for equality—not only in the wages they receive, but in ALL areas of employment, including status, promotion, benefits, and general terms of employment. Title VII is a comprehensive scheme designed to aid and assist women in attaining an equal footing with men. The right protected under the law is EQUAL TREATMENT. It is a law of comparability between similarly situated males and females in the workforce.

The educational field has been no exception to the ongoing discrimination against women in the workforce. There is a wide disparity in the total number of women employed in education and the percentage of those women who have attained the higher-level positions. Many argue that those who deserve to be promoted and rewarded are, that those who are not deserving remain at the lower levels, that there is no sex discrimination in educational employment but only an honest recognition of true merit. But employment statistics which indicate highly disproportionate representation of females in high-level positions constitute strong evidence of discriminatory practices. It seems unlikely that so few qualified women are employed by educational institutions, especially with such a high percentage of female workers.

An understanding of this employment problem in education can be gained from further reading of Title VII and the various regulations and guidelines interpreting it. Title VII recognizes that there are two types of discrimination today: intentional and unintentional. *Intentional* discrimination means that an employer consciously and willfully made an employment decision strictly on the basis of sex. Defining this type of discrimination is simple, but it can be difficult to prove in practice, particularly in demonstrating intent. It is virtually impossible to show the intent—the state of mind—of the employer when making an employment decision. Furthermore, with the abundance of laws now protecting employees, employers are well aware of their legal obligations and have become less overt in their discriminatory actions.

But while overt discrimination may have declined to some extent, employment discrimination persists through seemingly unintentional policies and practices that perpetuate the effects of past discriminatory acts. *Unintentional* discrimination is today the basis for the majority of complaints filed against employers by women. In an unintentional discrimination charge, it is not necessary to show the motives or intent of the employer. In these cases, it is only necessary to demonstrate the effect of the employer's practices that becomes important. It is the *consequences* of employment practices, not the *intent,* which determines whether discrimination exists.

The majority of school boards, administrative bodies, and decision-making bodies in today's educational institutions continue to be largely comprised of men. With the lack of representation of women in these decision-making bodies, there is a very real possibility for the unintentional, subtle forms of discrimination to occur. Employment decisions can be made for a variety of reasons which result in a discriminatory impact upon the women of the school or university. These underlying reasons can be ideas such as class stereotypes of women, old-fashioned beliefs as to what is best for the institution, and a feeling of satisfaction and security in continuing to operate a school in the same fashion it has been operated for the last 10 years. When dealing with decision-making processes such as these, a woman is faced head-on with unintentional sex discrimination.

Unintentional discrimination occurs when an employment policy appears neutral on its face, but in application has an adverse impact on female employees. A prime example can be seen in the effect a school board's recruiting methods has on the women employed in a school system. If an employer is seeking a new high school principal for a large city high school, it may resort to its old tried and true method of locating a suitable person. That practice may include only interviewing candidates who have received a degree from a certain university. On its face this policy appears perfectly neutral, but if that university is predominantly male, it is highly likely that a male will be chosen for the job. Very few women will be recruited or considered for the job and, in effect, women are kept out of the upper-level positions within that school system.

Women in higher education have traditionally held lower-level positions and are less often advanced to the upper-ranks of full professor or department heads. The university, in developing its guidelines for promotion, may impose requirements which are unrelated to ability but, more important, are impossible for the female members of the staff to meet. The requirements in and of themselves are not discriminatory perhaps, but only become so when the *effect* of the employment practice is analyzed. If the impact on female staff is a disparate one, they may constitute a violation of Title VII.

Employment statistics indicate that there continues to be a highly disproportionate representation of females in certain job categories. Title VII prohibits an employer from discriminating against women on the basis of sex in *employment opportunities.* Along this line, the U.S. Supreme Court has viewed Title VII as a vehicle to expand the role of women in the labor market and to do away with traditional stereotypes. Historically, certain jobs have been classified as suitable for women only because they required "feminine" or "ladylike" traits. Jobs traditionally viewed as male—heavy labor, skilled trades, coaching—were all but closed to women prior to Title VII. The Supreme Court has stated that Title VII rejects "romantic paternalism" of job stereotypes as "unduly Victorian" and, further, that Title VII gives women the power to decide whether to take on unromantic tasks.

An employer faced with an employment discrimination charge often tries to raise a defense of bona fide occupational qualification or "business necessity" for the discriminatory act. In the early days of the Civil Rights Act there was a great degree of latitude in using this defense—almost any reasonable grounds for an employment defense were upheld as bona fide occupational qualifications. Today, however, the courts have interpreted "business necessity" very narrowly and limited its use to only a few employment situations. For instance, if a job involves close personal contact with members of the opposite sex, perhaps in some gym classes, employers are allowed· to classify the position on the basis of sex. Beyond jobs which involve close personal contact, the courts have usually allowed the defense in situations where the physical attributes of maleness or femaleness are crucial, as in modeling or acting careers.

Employers may not use customer (student) preference, cost of hiring, or their own stereotyped perceptions of a woman's role in the work force in attempting to prove a bona fide occupational qualification. For example, if an employer only allows males to teach courses in finance or business because he believes men have a better aptitude for those courses, he is guilty of discrimination against women who desire to teach those courses. There is no bona fide business reason justifying only men teaching business courses.

Many employers have tried to claim that the increased cost of providing equal employment opportunities is a proper basis for the business necessity defense. The courts have expressly ruled that an employer cannot discriminate against women simply because it will cost more to employ them. For instance, if a school system employs only male janitors and maintenance personnel because the headquarters for those employees only has facilities for males, the cost of installing separate facilities for women will not be sufficient reason for denying women the opportunity of working in the maintenance department.

In narrowly interpreting the bona fide occupational qualification defense, the courts have recognized that to allow employers to claim a business necessity justification for discriminating against women would be to perpetuate the past discriminatory practices of that employer against women as a whole. To allow these past discriminatory practices to continue would circumvent the purpose of Title VII—equality for all workers.

Other Laws
Applying to Employment Discrimination

State Laws

As already noted, Title VII of the Civil Rights Act of 1964 is the primary protection against employment discrimination. The agency having enforcement authority of this law is the Equal Employment Opportunity Commission (EEOC). Title VII has also served as the model for states in passing their own fair employment laws. Understanding the provisions of Title VII insures that a woman knows what her rights are under federal law, but she must also learn about her rights under state law.

All but six of the states have adopted anti-discrimination in employment laws. The six states which have not passed comprehensive anti-discrimination laws are: Alabama, Arkansas, Louisiana, Mississippi, North Carolina and North Dakota. Women in these states will have to rely solely on Title VII as the enforcement vehicle in asserting a claim of sex discrimination in employment. It should be noted that these six states do have some employment laws, which vary from state to state, and it is possible that these states will in the future pass employment laws which will be as comprehensive as Title VII. Therefore, any woman residing in one of these six states should try to keep informed as to any current or pending legislation in the area of fair employment practices.

The remainder of the states have anti-discrimination laws which are comparable to Title VII. These laws vary from state to state as to the comprehensiveness of the law, as well as the procedural requirements and standards of proofs. While based on Title VII, they differ somewhat in the amount of protection granted working women, as well as in the relief available to the injured woman.

Because both state and federal laws exist which protect working women, jurisdiction over discrimination complaints is said to be *concurrent* — the state and federal governments both have enforcement authority at the same time. Because employment problems are local in nature, the federal government has agreed to allow the states to have the first opportunity to resolve any employment problems within that state by first using state law. In order to allow states this first chance at solving discrimination problems, the EEOC has entered into contracts with these states for state agencies to handle the complaints originating in that state. These agencies are known as "706 deferral agencies" and are set forth in Appendix A.

When a state has attained the status of a "706 state," an employee is required to first file with that agency before seeking any action on the part of the federal government. What this means to a woman with a sex discrimination complaint is that she must first file with the 706 agency in her state and have her complaint interpreted under the state law.

Many of the states have not yet developed clear-cut guidelines as to their agency's procedures and practices when a complaint is filed with it. Each state, as already noted, has its own procedural requirements, the most important being that of *when* a complaint must be filed. The federal rule allows a complaint to be filed within 180 days of a discriminatory act. States vary on this requirement, ranging from 60 days to 300 days.

While Title VII provides for deferral to states for a first attempt at solving any discrimination in employment problems, it also provides that a woman may appeal any decision of a state agency to the EEOC, in which case federal law, Title VII, will be used in deciding the complaint. However, if a state has a filing time of 300 days within the occurrence of a discriminatory act, and a woman files her complaint on the 200th day, she has already gone beyond the

180 days under the federal rule, but has satisfied her state's requirement. Title VII specifically provides that, in this case, the woman would still have a right to bring her case to the EEOC on appeal if the complaint is filed with the EEOC within 300 days of the discrimination, and if the complaint were timely filed in the state action. Even with this exception to the time for filing a complaint, the woman would have to be certain that her complaint is ultimately filed with the EEOC within 300 days of the act complained of.

A converse problem is seen in states which have less than 180 days as a time limitation. For example, if a state requires that a complaint be filed within 60 days of an unfair employment practice and a woman attempts to file on the 80th day, she MAY be rejected by the state. However, she still has a right to file with the EEOC without going through her state agency. This right accures because, in effect, the deferral agency has refused to accept jurisdiction over the matter. Many women have lost perfectly valid complaints because, when refused by the 706 agency for late filing, they assumed that they could not file with the EEOC.

Another area of possible confusion is when a state 706 Deferral Agency defers its jurisdiction over certain matters back to the EEOC. For example, a state may decide that any cases involving discrimination because of pregnancy will be deferred to the federal government. This release of jurisdiction by the state must be approved by the EEOC. In the event a state has limited its jurisdiction, a woman files directly with the EEOC as to those specified matters.

The interplay between state and federal law and the effect of state procedural requirements on a sex discrimination complaint is the most confusing area of Title VII. There are no national guidelines for states to use in handling sex discrimination complaints, and the danger is very great that a valid complaint could be lost because of bureaucratic confusion and misapplication of the various laws involved. Most attorneys agree that the most valuable service they perform for a client is ensuring that the complaint is filed with the appropriate agency within the allotted time. If only for this reason, a woman is wise to consult with an attorney when planning to file a sex discrimination complaint. Because they are so crucial to a successful case, the various time requirements and filing procedures are discussed more fully in Chapter IV.

Title IX

As employees of institutions receiving federal funds, most women in education have an additional protective law which is quite powerful in getting their administration's attention. This law is known as Title IX and prohibits discrimination on the basis of sex in institutions receiving federal funds. Essentially, the only educational institutions not covered by Title IX are religious and military schools.

The provisions and protections of Title IX are patterned after Title VII insofar as they relate to employment practices. The protection is very comprehensive, with the only real drawback to Title IX being in the type of relief offered.

Under Title IX, the only remedy provided for is the withdrawal of federal funds to the involved institution. The complaining employee receives no remuneration, but does receive a cessation of any discriminatory practices on the part of the employer. Although this is the ultimate goal when filing a sex discrimination complaint, most women also desire some settlement for their time, energy and money spent in pursuing an equal employment opportunity claim.

Title IX should be viewed as an ancillary weapon in pursuing a remedy for sex discrimination in employment. Many lawyers who have handled discrimination claims for women in education have noticed a remarkable change in attitude when the woman files under Title IX. They observe that when a complaint is filed under Title VII, many school administrators adopt the attitude of "waiting it out" to see who will break first, before conceding to any discriminatory practices. But when a claim is filed under Title IX, the administrators attempt to settle the matter as quickly as possible. After all, without federal funds supporting their institution, there will be very little for them to do. Therefore, in order to avoid even the possibility of losing any federal monies, the administration becomes very serious about resolving the problem at hand.

A complaint under Title IX is filed with the Department of Education in Washington, D.C. Once a complaint is filed with the Department, the female employee is relieved of any further active role in the action. The Department will undertake its own investigation and, based upon its findings, will make a final determination. Therefore, it is important that the woman supply as much information as possible when she files her complaint. The more data the Department of Education has when it initiates its investigation, the quicker a decision will be made. It is possible through the Freedom of Information Act to secure a copy of the employer's answer to the complaint. If any errors or omissions are discovered, they should be reported to the Department.

Strategically, any woman employed by an educational institution receiving federal funds should file both under Title VII and Title IX. This makes the employer aware of the seriousness of the charged offenses, and of how serious the employee is in receiving relief.

A word of warning is required as to filing Title IX complaints which allege discriminatory practices. There is a trend by some of the federal courts to rule that Title IX is not intended to protect the rights of employees in educational institutions. Rather, these courts feel that Title IX is designed to protect only the rights of *recipients* of federal funds, i.e., students. These cases have not been tested in the Supreme Court yet, so there is no firm rule regarding these decisions. A recent Court of Appeals case held that *employees* were covered under Title IX. It remains to be seen if the U.S. Supreme Court will hear this matter on appeal. Women employed in the educational field should continue to attempt to file Title IX complaints to protect themselves in the event the issue is resolved in favor of the teachers and other female employees in education.

Equal Pay Act

There is another law today which has limited authority in preventing sex discrimination in employment. The Equal Pay Act was created specifically to outlaw discriminatory wages being paid to men and women performing the same services. This law prohibits a woman being paid less than a man performing similar work for the sole reason that she is a woman.

On July 1, 1979, the EEOC was given enforcement authority of the Equal Pay Act. Prior to that time, the Department of Labor had been in charge of enforcing the act. The enforcement of the Act was transferred to the EEOC in an effort to consolidate the handling of cases involving sex discrimination.

Because the EEOC has had authority to enforce the Act for such a short length of time, many questions have not been answered as to the approach the EEOC will take in resolving unequal pay complaints. The Department of Labor

had taken the position that in order to prove a claim of unequal pay on the basis of sex, the employee had to show that
she had equal skill, responsibility, effort and similar working
conditions to her male counterpart, and that she was paid
less. At times this standard of proof has been overwhelming
to a complaining employee. Trying to prove equal skill, responsibility, effort and similar working conditions involved
many subjective criteria, which were not easily classified or
categorized. The result was that many women could not meet
the standard of proof and lost their Equal Pay Act complaints.

The EEOC has always been in disagreement with the
Department of Labor's standard of proof. In deciding a complaint of unequal pay under Title VII, they use a standard of
proof of a similarly situated or comparable male employee
or one whose work is of comparable worth. This standard
has a far more liberal application, and allows a complaining
employee to show many more factors than just skill, responsibility and effort. The result has been that, under Title VII,
far more women were able to successfully prove discrimination in wages on the basis of sex.

Another area of difference between the Department of
Labor and the EEOC in pay differential cases is that of procedure. Prior to the transfer of enforcement authority to the
EEOC, the procedure was quite simple. A woman merely
had to file a complaint with the Department of Labor claiming she was not receiving equal pay for equal work and the
Department took over from there. The woman was not actively involved once the complaint was filed.

Under EEOC procedure there is more likelihood that the woman will remain actively involved with the case. However, as of the date of this publication there have been no guidelines issued by the EEOC as to their policies in enforcing the Equal Pay Act. It is not certain whether the EEOC will maintain the simplicity of Equal Pay violation complaints, or whether they will follow the more complicated procedure involved in filing a Title VII complaint.

Because of the ease of procedure, women used to file a complaint under the Equal Pay Act instead of Title VII when the only discriminatory act was that of pay. Now, until the EEOC issues guidelines regarding their practice and procedure when the Equal Pay Act is involved, a woman will have to contact her regional EEOC office, set out in Appendix B, and discuss her problem with an agency representative.

"Shotgun" Approach

While this book deals solely with sex discrimination in employment, there are other protective laws under which a woman may file an unfair employment practice complaint. Title VII specifically prohibits discrimination in employment on the basis of race, color, religion, sex, or national origin. Additionally, there are laws which prohibit discrimination in employment on the basis of handicap or age.

If a woman is being discriminated against on the basis of her sex, as well as her race, handicap, religious beliefs, age or nationality, she should consider filing a multi-faceted complaint.

This is often referred to as the "shotgun" approach, alleging each and every discriminatory act, not just those based on sex, and filing with all of the appropriate agencies. This approach has become easier since the EEOC now handles almost all complaints involving discriminatory employment practices.

The shotgun approach is actually a preferred method of filing, as the EEOC and courts prefer that all complaints an employee may have against an employer be aired at one time and resolved in one proceeding, rather than stringing the complaints out over a number of months or even years. This is not to say that a woman should concoct or create additional discriminatory practices if in fact she is only being discriminated against because of her sex. Groundless or unwarranted allegations will hurt, more than aid, other valid allegations. To make irresponsible charges regarding one employment practice tends to reflect badly on other valid and worthy complaints.

There are many advantages to this shotgun-type of filing. The woman assures that all of her rights will be protected, she saves time in the long run by preparing one complaint, she saves in attorney fees, and most important, there will be one proceeding and one resolution as to all her problems.

Remedies Provided By the Law

Pursuing a discrimination claim can prove to be quite costly to the employee. However, the expenses incurred may be far outweighed by the remedies obtained in successfully proving the charge.

A wide spectrum of relief is available to the employee, with the courts and EEOC having discretionary authority in the granting of any or all relief. What this means is that the employee could receive back wages, reinstatement, injunctions against the employer, or a combination of these, plus others as set out below.

The most sought after relief is generally that of back pay. The granting of back pay is a direct remedy to the employee — monetary compensation for the discriminatory acts of the employer. Back pay can be awarded for a period of up to two years prior to the filing of a charge of sex discrimination. However, if there is intentional conduct on the part of the employer in the discriminatory practices, the employee may be able to receive up to three years back pay from the date of filing the complaint.

Back wages are computed by determining what the employee actually received and what she would have received had there been no discrimination involved. The difference is the amount the employee will receive. If the employee was passed over for a promotion because she is a woman, then the difference in pay would be what she would have received, if promoted, less what she actually received.

In a case involving discharge of a female employee for discriminatory reasons, the employee will be entitled to receive the compensation she would have earned if she had not been discharged. However, the employee must make a good faith attempt to find a new job within the same category of her prior employment. The employee is not required to seek out employment in any area, but she must look for employment in the same or similar type of position she previously held. If the employee's discharge is found to be one based on discriminatory practices, the employer may be required to reinstate the employee, as well as pay her back wages.

In situations involving on-going discriminatory practices, such as a lack of female employees in a position as compared to the number of men in the same position, the employer may be required by way of injunction to implement an affirmative action program. Injunctive relief can be granted in cases involving promotion policies, benefit plans, hiring practices, or any practice of the employer which has an adverse impact on women and is not justified by a bona fide business necessity. The injunction may order the employer to immediately stop its discriminatory practices, as well as order the development of affirmative action plans. The EEOC or the courts, in granting injunctive relief, will be using the facts found to exist in the complaining employee's charge as a basis to prevent the reoccurrence or continuance of the discriminatory practices of the employer.

Overcontributions to pension plans or retirement programs may be reimbursed to the female employee and, in addition, interest may be awarded at the current legal rate so as to compensate the woman for money which could have been earned through investment.

The granting of attorney fees to an employee who successfully proves a discrimination charge is generally recognized in court actions. The allowing of attorney fees is highly discretionary and there is some split among the courts as to what constitutes fair and just attorney fees. Attorney fees may be denied to the employee where her attorney's incompetence or inaction led to the fees incurred. However, in most cases where the employee is the winning party, some type of settlement may be made for the employer to reimburse the employee's attorney.

The trend today is to allow attorney fees only in court actions, but there is a growing tendency of the court to order payment of the employee's attorney fees in proceedings before the Equal Employment Opportunity Commission. One federal court has even ordered the payment of attorney fees in a state administrative proceeding. However, this case has not yet been appealed and the validity of the decision remains to be tested by the higher courts. The granting of attorney fees at the administrative level is tenuous at best. The courts which have granted fees in agency proceedings have expressed the theory that a complaining employee should have benefit of counsel at the agency level where legal advice is often crucial and that the inability to afford legal counsel could have a detrimental effect on subsequent court proceedings. The courts have also indicated that it is highly desirable to have discrimination cases resolved at the agency level and that the presence of counsel could, perhaps, lead to quicker and more satisfactory resolution of the charge.

A charge of sex discrimination usually involves more than just one issue, and therefore the type and amount of relief varies from case to case. The drafting of the original complaint will be crucial in that the more discriminatory acts alleged, the more the employee may receive. However, an employee may not frivilously submit a charge containing numerous allegations in the hopes of receiving the greatest amount of relief possible. All complaints must be made in good faith and the relief the employee ultimately receives will be based on the findings of the appropriate agency or court.

Protection From Reprisal and Retaliation

To prevent adverse employer reaction toward an employee who complains of discrimination under Title VII, certain protections are provided. Harassment of the charging employee, denial of benefits, disciplinary actions or other forms of retaliation and reprisal by the employer are forbidden by Title VII.

These protective measures were created to prevent a frustration of Title VII where the employer would be able to make unilateral decisions as to the truth or falsity of the charges made. If the employer had such an unfettered right, it would have an extremely chilling effect on the employee in her decision whether to assert her legal rights.

The guarantees of freedom from reprisal and retaliation by the employer under Title VII come into play in two situations: first where the employee has *opposed* an unlawful employment practice, and second where the employee has *participated* in any administrative proceeding against the employment practices of the employer. In the situation where the woman has opposed an unlawful employment practice, some problems of interpretation arise. Opposing a practice does not necessarily include filing of any charges with an administrative agency or a court. Opposition can include protesting to the employer, or discussing the employment practice with other co-workers. The question of how much protection will be given a woman who only opposes a practive without pursuing legal actions is answered by two different theories.

The EEOC and the courts have sharply differing opinions as to when Title VII protection will be given in an opposition situation. The courts generally believe that in order for a woman to be protected from reprisals and retaliation, she must show that she opposed a practice which *in fact existed* and which equaled a violation of Title VII. The EEOC follows the theory that protection will be granted if the employee *reasonably believed* an employment practice existed which, if true, equaled a Title VII violation.

These two theories differ drastically in their outcomes. The following situations show how. In the first, *A,* a female non-tenured university professor, learns that *B,* a male she believes comparable in qualifications to herself, has been granted tenure instead of her, although *A* has repeatedly requested tenure be granted to her. *A* protests vigorously to the various administrators to no avail. *A* then decides to inform all the women faculty members that the university is discriminating against her. As it turns out, the male employee was entitled to tenure and the woman really wasn't. If the employer reprimands her in some fashion and she claims the reprisal violates Title VII, two outcomes are possible.

If the woman's complaint is heard before a court, the court will, in all likelihood, deny her claim of retaliation. The simple reason is that no employment practice existed which was a violation of Title VII. The employer did not discriminate against the woman in denying tenure. In effect, the courts are requiring that a woman make an accurate legal determination regarding the lawfulness of the employer's action before opposing it. For this reason, the employee should take every precaution before opposing an employment practice if she is not going to file a complaint with a proper agency or authority.

If the claim is heard by the EEOC, the outcome would probably be the opposite. If *A* REASONABLY believed she had been discriminated against, the EEOC would grant relief to the employee for any injury she suffered because of the employer's reprisals. All the woman would have to prove is that she honestly and in good faith believed her charge of discrimination and that if it had been proven, the practice would have been a violation of Title VII.

The difference in the two theories is the amount of knowledge the opposing party has. Under the courts' view, the employee must know with certainty that the employer's practice was prohibited under Title VII. The EEOC only requires that she reasonably believed the employer's act was a violation of Title VII. The EEOC only weeds out opposition practices which are arbitrary, frivolous, or vindictive. The court's position will deny relief to any woman reprimanded for opposing a practice which, in the end result, was not an unlawful employment practice.

The second situation in which sanctions will be imposed for reprisals by the employer is when the employee files or participates in a complaint of discrimination that has been filed with an appropriate administrative agency. This protection extends not only to the charging party, but also covers employees who testify in any administrative or court proceedings. Participation, under Title VII, includes sending letters to the EEOC or state agency requesting information or advice or filing requests for data about the employer.

When retaliation is made against an employee because of participation in Title VII proceedings, a very broad interpretation of statutory sanctions is made. Both the courts and

EEOC recognize that each and every employee must be assured of complete access to Title VII and the protections guaranteed under it.

In this case, when claiming retaliation by the employer, the employee need not prove the validity of her claim of sex discrimination. She only needs to show that the complaint was filed in good faith, and that she reasonably believes in the validity of her charge. The Supreme Court has stated that where accusations are made in the context of a charge before the EEOC, the truth or falsity of the accusations must be determined by the EEOC. This is an important difference from the court's belief in cases involving retaliation because of opposition to an employment practice.

One explanation for the difference in theories is that Congress has created legal machinery for an employee to use in employment situations which may be in violation of Title VII. Because the legal tool exists to amicably settle employment relationship problems, the courts want to encourage their use, i.e. filing complaints as opposed to "self-help."

Additionally, the laws guaranteeing women certain employment rights do not give the female employee a license to disrupt the employer's organization. Legal recourse is available for the airing of all complaints. Title VII proceedings are the proper forum for settlement of disputes and the courts will vigorously defend the right to use that forum.

Procedural rules require that a charging party file a complaint of reprisal or retaliation *immediately*. There should be as little time lapse as possible between the retaliatory act and the filing of the charge.

The affected employee will need to show the adverse employment practice and prove there is a causal connection between that act and the filing of the sex discrimination complaint. If the employee proves the causal connection, the employer will be severely sanctioned. The EEOC has wide discretion in the type of punishment, but will generally try to compensate the employee as fully as possible.

If the employee was unlawfully laid off, she could be reinstated and receive lost wages. An employer may have to compensate the woman for harassment she had to endure. The EEOC would probably arrive at a dollar amount which they felt was adequate compensation. An injunction could also be issued ordering the employer to stop all retaliatory acts. These are just a few examples of the variety of remedies available in a retaliation claim.

All employees are protected under the laws when alleging unlawful employment practices. However, the law requires the employee to make her allegations in good faith and upon reasonable grounds. Frivilous or unwarranted claims by an employee will weight heavily against her in any subsequent proceedings alleging retaliation or reprisal by the employer.

Chapter III
SOME MAJOR ISSUES
IN EDUCATIONAL EMPLOYMENT

Sex-Plus Discrimination

A general principle for deteriming whether a particular employment practice is discriminatory is referred to as sex-plus. Sex-plus discrimination occurs when the employer bases an employment decision on sex, plus one additional factor, and where that factor is applied to only one sex. An example of sex-plus discrimination would be refusing to hire a woman because she has pre-school age children but hiring a man with pre-school age children.

In reviewing sex-plus cases, the courts have looked to see whether the employment decision was based on factors in addition to sex. These factors may be categorized as either immutable and mutable characteristics.

Immutable characteristics are simply those which are unchangeable due to the fact that an individual is female. A typical case of this type might be the refusal to hire women because they are physically unable to lift as much as a man. According to the law, an employer may not base an employment decision on any immutable characteristics of women, and this type of sex-plus discrimination is becoming quite rare. In the field of education it is even more unlikely that an employee will ever encounter a situation where she is being discriminated against because she is a woman, plus some immutable characteristic.

The area where there is the greatest abuse by employers involves *mutable* characteristics, those which are changeable but are associated with a particular sex. Some mutable characteristics have also been determined to be fundamental rights. To date, the courts have decided that only the right to marry and the right to have children are fundamental rights protected by the law.

The issue of married female employees was first decided in the cases involving airline stewardesses. The airline involved had a policy against employing married female stewardesses, but not against married male stewards. The court found that marriage was a personal right and employers could not justify an employment practice of a "no-marriage" rule, unless there was a bona fide business necessity. The court further indicated that it would be extremely difficult to show that marital status was really a business necessity. The court felt that the marital status of an employee has very little relevance to that employee's ability or inability to perform a job properly.

Denying a woman employment, or firing her, because she has children is also in violation of Title VII. An employer could only impose such a prohibition against women if it also applied to male employees. The courts have recognized that the right to marry and the right to have children are rights which cannot be denied or restrained because of unfair employment practices.

Certain mutable characteristics are not provided any protection under the law. For example, an employer may regulate the type of dress the employee must wear, the length of hair, the amount of make-up, etc. The courts have interpreted Title VII as affording protection to the fundamental rights to marry and have children, but they have not extended Title VII or other laws to protect those changeable, although personal, characteristics of an employee. The courts have held that Congressional intent in passing Title VII was to grant equal access to the job market to both sexes, but not to completely limit an employer's discretion in how best to run his business.

It is important to remember that Title VII is only violated on a sex-plus basis when one sex is being required to meet additional criteria, such as not having children. If only women have to meet this employment requirement, while men do not, there is a violation of Title VII.

Compensation

At the heart of Title VII is the provision that the terms and conditions of employment shall be the same for all employees. One of the terms of employment most important to an employee is generally her wage or salary.

Inequities in pay scales still exist. The educational field, with its high percentage of female employees, is a prime example of continuing unequal pay rates for women.

Employment as a teacher or professor carries many chances for arbitrary and capricious action on the part of the employer. The standards used in determining pay scales for educators are subject to undefinable criteria because they involve characteristics and qualities which are not well suited for neat categorization. Because the profession is so highly dependent upon the qualities of the individual instructor, the possibility for differing wages among men and women is great.

According to law, an employer, when determining pay scales, must not use arbitrary methods of classifying employees. The standards for pay scales set by the employer must reasonably relate to the job classification and requisite skill, knowledge and ability. However, many educational employers may still attempt to justify different salaries for male and female employees by hiding behind superfluous reasons.

The EEOC has recognized that some employers may use ambiguous job classifications and descriptions when setting pay scales and subjects these classifications to very close scrutiny when a charge of pay discrimination on the basis of sex has been filed against an employer.

The ideal situation for proving sex discrimination in pay would be to have a male and female employee who were identical in every respect, except for their sex. It would be next to impossible for an employer to refute a discrimination charge where the male receives a larger salary, and the female employee is essentially the same employee.

Creating this comparable male can be difficult. Especially if the educational institution or school system involved is a small one. If there are few male employees, it may be difficult to pick one which matches the qualifications and abilities of the woman. There are a number of ways to solve this problem of proof and finding a comparable male model.

In deciding whether the male and female employees are similar, or similarly situated, the EEOC and courts will use a balancing approach in weighing the merits of each employee and his/her job. This balancing allows a female employee a chance to prove a discriminatory employment practice by weighing her values and merits against similar values and merits of a male employee. For example, if a woman instructor had a Ph.D. in Sociology, taught three classes to senior students, had been employed for 4 years and had the status of associate professor, she may be able to compare herself to a male employee who had only 3 years of service with the employer, taught 3 classes to junior students, also had the status of associate professor, and had a Ph.D. in History. Both are teachers in the College of Liberal Arts. They are not exactly the same, but there is enough similarity between them to claim that the male involved is indeed a comparable male.

As a general rule, a woman may use as her standard of proof a male employee who is not as qualified, knowledgeable, etc. as she but who receives more than she does for the same work. An employer will be hard-pressed to support a lower salary for a female employee who is better qualified, in a better position with the employer, or who has more responsibilities than a male employee in the same department.

In creating the comparable male, it is important that the male employee be within the same school, department, division or area as the female teacher. At the university and college level, a female instructor in the Language Department would not use a male in the Physical Education Department as her comparable counterpart. At the elementary level, the woman should attempt to find a male who teaches at the same level. She should not compare a kindergarten teacher to herself if she were a 9th grade teacher. There would be too much room for argument that the two employees were not the same. If, however, the employer compensates employees in a predominantly male department at a higher rate, a claim may well be made.

In order to have a valid comparable male there must be some common factors between the man and woman. These factors should be as narrowly drawn as possible and subject to easy documentation, i.e. paper credentials. For example, if a woman has earned a Ph.D., she should compare herself to other Ph.D.s within her department. If a woman is a basketball coach, she should compare herself to male basketball coaches. If a secretary is being paid less than a male administrative assistant, she would rely on the closeness of the job descriptions and responsibilities with a disparity in pay.

A charge of discriminatory pay practices can be further strengthened by the use of department-by-department or school-wide evaluations of the pay to men and to women. By doing this, a woman will be able to create a larger picture to show a discriminatory pattern in pay scales by the employer. Although the primary proof used will be the comparable male, this in-depth type of analysis can be invaluable in proving discrimination on the part of the employer.

In proving her claim of sex discrimination in the payment of wages, a woman must be prepared to thoroughly explain her job, as well as the job of her comparable male, and also to present a competent comparable male. She must become intimate with her employer's wage practices and policies, and be prepared to meet any argument the employer may have as to why she is paid less than her male counterpart. The use of the comparable male, as well as an in-depth analysis of the employer's practices in regard to the school or university, will greatly help in preparing to rebut any arguments the employer may present.

Fringe Benefits

Fringe benefits, under Title VII, include medical, hospital, accident, and life insurance and retirement benefits, profit-sharing and bonus plans. It is a violation of Title VII to discriminate between men and women with regard to fringe benefits. Discrimination in the benefits area includes denying certain benefits to one sex, requiring only one sex to pay for benefits, having different benefits depending on the sex of an employee or imposing arbitrary requirements in order to qualify for benefits.

Equality in benefits means the employer will be faced with an increased cost in the provision of fringe benefits. This additional cost has been used by employers in the past to defend inequalities in benefit programs. The courts have ruled, however, that additional cost factors are not a proper defense in a discrimination charge. Regardless of the expense, an employer must provide equal benefits to all employees.

When the additional cost defense failed to work, employers then tried to condition the receipt of benefits on classifications of employees as "head of household" or "principal wage earner" of the family. This tactic has also been held to be a violation of Title VII. Such classification was held to be discriminatory because it adversely affected the rights of women employees and, further, the status as principal wage earner or head of household bore no relationship to an individual's job performance.

Today, if any benefit plan carries those restrictions— head of household or principal wage earner—the plan will be found to be a *prima facie* (on its face) violation of the prohibitions against sex discrimination under Title VII. The importance of this is largely procedural. If the employee shows that the benefit package carries these illegal classes, she will have to go no further. More important, the employer will have no defenses available. The mere existence of the requirements will render the plan illegal as being discriminatory, and the affected employee will be entitled to relief from the administrative agency or court.

Married working women are often covered by their husband's hospitalization and medical insurance. Ordinarily, an employer cannot refuse to cover the married female employee simply because she is taken care of under her husband's policy. However, if the employer also refuses benefits to a male employee covered under his wife's plan, there would be uniformity of application in benefits and most likely no discrimination.

It is also an unlawful employment practice for an employer to provide or make available benefits to the wives and families of male employees where the same benefits are not made available to the husbands and families of female employees. The overriding theme is equality—all employees must be treated the same, and this extends to the privileges conferred upon the families of employees.

When the employee must contribute to benefit packages, for instance when the employer pays a percentage of the total cost and the employee pays the remainder, male and female employees must be assessed equal contributions. A female employee cannot be required to pay a larger percentage than her male counterpart.

The benefit subject to the greatest controversy is that of retirement program or pension plan. The controversy arises because of the long-accepted use of acturarial tables in determining the amount of contribution and monthly benefits received based on life expectancy. Statistically, women as a group have a longer life span than men. Because statistics show women live to an older age, employers have either required a woman to contribute the same and receive a smaller monthly pension or to contribute more and receive the same monthly benefit as male retirees. The argument advanced by employers was that statistically the disproportionate payments or contributions would eventually equalize because women as a class outlive men.

The benchmark case of *City of Los Angeles v Manhart*, 435 US 702 (1978) put an end to part of the retirement benefits debate. *Manhart* involved the situation of female employees making larger contributions to the retirement fund and receiving less in monthly benefits upon retirement than male employees. The City of Los Angeles based their defense on the contributions on acturarial tables showing a longer life expectancy of women, thereby justifying the extra contributions on a factor other than sex, i.e. longevity. The City also argued that any differences in contributions were offset by the benefits received. The City claimed that because of the longer lives of women, they would receive more in benefits than men.

In holding the retirement scheme to be in violation of Title VII, the court emphasized the necessity of treating employees as individuals and not as members of a class. A true generalization about the class, according to the court, would not even be sufficient reason for disqualifying an individual to whom the generalization does not apply. Many women do live longer, but many women also live the same number of years, or fewer years than men. Because an individual's death is impossible to predetermine, the City argued it would be unfair to its male employees to require equal contributions. This sense of fairness was determined by the court to be a matter for legislative decision. In the absence of any such legislation, the court felt Title VII explicitly prohibited contribution differentials to pension/retirement plans on the basis of a class characterization, i.e. the statistical life span of a group of employees (women).

The opinion given by the Supreme Court was limited to unequal contributions. The question of equal contributions, but unequal monthly payments was not directly addressed. However, the court did indicate that, "Nothing in our holding implies that it would be unlawful for an employer to set aside equal retirement contributions for each employee and let each retiree purchase the largest benefit which his or her accumulated contributions could command in the open market."

The EEOC has issued guidelines requiring both equal contributions and equal benefits. However, these agency guidelines have not yet been tested by the Supreme Court. The current view of employers and most federal and state agencies is that equal contributions and unequal benefits will be within the limits of Title VII requirements.

Retirement age for male and female employees must also be the same. An employer cannot require a woman to retire at an earlier age than a man unless there is a justified business necessity for so doing. In one case, a woman was required to retire at age 62, while men could wait until age 65 to retire. The woman sued under Title VII, proved discrimination, and was awarded the three years pay she would have received between ages 62 and 65.

Vesting rights must also be the same for men and women. The employer cannot have separate criteria for women to meet in order for retirement/pension benefits to vest. The same seniority criteria or other standards must be applied equally to all employees. A female employee who realizes she is being discriminated against in the vesting provisions established by her employer and wants to pursue the problem without filing an EEOC complaint does have an avenue open to her. The Internal Revenue Code, Section 411, prohibits discriminatory vesting provisions and any violation may be reported to the Internal Revenue Service for resolution. The woman involved should contact her local IRS office for additional guidance.

Tenure and Promotion

Separate lines of progression and seniority systems for men and women are expressly prohibited by Title VII. This means that an employer may not have one set of standards for men to meet in order to advance in their employment, and another standard for women. Criteria established by the employer for either promotion or tenure must apply equally to all employees. The specific qualifications and standards an employee must meet in order to be promoted or to be granted tenure are determined by the employer and are within the employer's discretion. However, this discretion is not absolute.

The employer may not create artificial barriers in career advancement in order to keep women at lower levels of the hierarchy of the organization. The criteria for promotion/ tenure set by an employer are subject to close scrutiny by the EEOC and courts. In reviewing promotion/tenure requirements, the EEOC and courts will determine whether the qualifications are reasonably related to the job in question.

By imposing unrelated job requrements, an employer may be in violation of Title VII—for example, requiring a Ph.D. in Early Childhood Development for a high school principal. Undoubtedly a Ph.D. in early childhood development would be an asset to a high school principal, but is it necessary to perform competently as a principal? This Ph.D. requirement appears neutral on its face, but its application may reveal a severe discriminatory motive. If there were ten applicants for the position as principal, nine women and one man, and only one—the man—had a Ph.D. in early childhood development, the argument could be made that the degree requirement was created for the sole purpose of making the man the only "qualified" applicant. This type of requirement has been called "illusory" by the courts. It appears to serve a valid purpose at first glance, but upon closer scrutiny, reveals a discriminatory motive.

Imposing illusory promotion/tenure standards is a common occurrence, especially in education. Although the total educational workforce is largely female, there is a marked decrease of women in supervisory, high-level administration or in upper-level teaching positions. Women in education who are being unjustly passed over for advancement or tenure face two problems: the attitude of the courts and the difficulty of proving unlawful promotion/tenure practices.

A federal court, in a 1975 case involving Tufts Institution of Learning, stated that evaluations for academic advancement can seldom be measured by mechanical processes or standardized tests. "If criteria are reasonably related to professional duties and to personal qualifications—statistics or membership in a protected class will be insufficient for an initial showing of discrimination." The mechanical processes mentioned by the court refer to the inability of an educational employer to set down clear-cut, precise, objective criteria for career advancement. The various positions within an educational institution are often unique in and of themselves, requiring particular skills, knowledge and expertise. For this reason, some federal courts have a tendency to give great weight to the decisions made by the administrators of the institution. The courts adopting this attitude believe that the requirements for promotion or tenure of an educator are highly subjective and that, because of the subjectivity, a unique relationship exists between the institution and the employee that should not be interfered with by the courts. Apparently these courts believe that there are too many unquantifiable requirements in an education job as compared to employment by a manufacturer or large corporation. The requirements the courts are concerned about are the highly individualized ones of personality, ability to relate with others, classroom rapport, student reactions and fellow faculty opinions. Essentially, the courts following these beliefs have created sanctuaries for possible discrimination of all types. These courts will only review promotion/tenure decisions where the employer acted "arbitrarily or unreasonably."

The EEOC does not share in these assumptions and maintains that the educational employer-employee relationship is no different from any other employer-employee relationship. There is also a trend for *some* federal courts to view educational institutions in the same way as any other employer. These courts have recognized that allowing educa-

tional systems such latitude in promotion/tenure decisions perpetuates archaic and discriminatory practices. Further, these courts believe that career advancement decisions by educational employers can be placed into objective terms and that reasonable standards for promotion and tenure can be implemented.

Once the female employee gets her case before the court, or EEOC, the issue of proofs becomes crucial. Because advancement requirements of an employer are discretionary and often highly subjective, the complaining employee will need to use statistics and a job analysis in proving her charge.

The EEOC requires both elementary and secondary schools, as well as institutions of higher education, to file certain forms with it. These forms can be invaluable to an employee in preparing her proofs in a promotion or tenure dispute.

Form EEO-5 applies to elementary and secondary schools. All school systems having more than 15 employees are required to file EEO-5, unless the school district can show an undue hardship in preparing and filing the report. The form summarizes data for *all* personnel employed, either full-time or part-time. The form first establishes activity classifications such as administrator, classroom teacher, clerical, skilled labor, professional staff, etc. The activity classifications are then broken down into male/female and then the male/female categories are broken down into race (Black, Hispanic, White, etc.). The report does not require salary disclosure, but it will give a comprehensive picture of the school system's utilization of personnel. It may be possible from the use of the information contained in the form to show how the employer has a definite pattern of few women in higher-level jobs, which could raise an inference of discrimination.

Institutions of higher education are required to file Form EEO-6. The institutions which must file are public and private schools, colleges and universities, community colleges, and junior colleges. The institutions also may plead undue hardship in preparing and filing the report and, if approved, be released from responsibility in filing. EEO-6 is more comprehensive than EEO-5 in that the form requires a breakdown of all personnel, either full-time or part-time, and then breaks the personnel down on the basis of occupational activity, salary and length of contract, either 9-10 month or 11-12 month contracts. Tenured and non-tenured on-track employees must also be indicated.

All educational employers are required to keep copies of the reports on file. This does not mean the employer will release the report to an employee, but the employee can file a request under the Freedom of Information Act, either with the employer, the EEOC, or with HEW, which receives copies also.

By using the information compiled from these forms, the employee may be able to show that the employer has a pattern of discrimination against women. Additional statistical information should also be prepared so that a comparison of the employer to other educational employers can be made. This can be accomplished by obtaining either the EEO-5 or EEO-6 of surrounding school systems or even attempting a regional, district or state-wide compilation of facts.

When trying to prove her case of discriminatory practices in promotion, the employee must also present evidence of a non-statistical nature. This is where a job analysis is important. By analyzing the job itself, it can be decided if the requirements for advancement to the job are really valid and reasonable. Also in reviewing the job requirements, the employee should be looking for any sex stereotyping (e.g. men make better math teachers) or criteria that favor men (e.g. requiring total flexibility in hours favors men over women with children because of child-rearing responsibilities). In doing the analysis, the employee should be aware of these subtle types of discrimination which were discussed in Chapter I. For instance, requiring a degree from a certain college in order to receive tenure may not be discriminatory, but it becomes discriminatory if the college is an all-male private college.

The issues of tenure and career advancement in education are volatile ones. Perhaps this area of discrimination is the one that will see the greatest changes in the coming years. The makeup of the members of either the administrative agency or the court the employee deals with will be crucial to her case. As changes are made in the membership of these agencies, it is likely that more people will sway to the theory that an educational employer is the same as any other. Although there is still widespread belief that an educational institution is an ivory tower and better left unbothered by outside interference, this belief is not an impossible hurdle to overcome and an employee should prepare herself to present an argument as to why the employer is like any other.

Even though the task may seem formidable, women in educational employment should not be discouraged. The Educational Amendments of 1972 were the first laws making educational institutions subject to Title VII and there have been few cases decided by the courts since that time. Because the novelty of sanctioning an educational employer is so new, there is plenty of room to argue in its favor.

Pregnancy and Child-Rearing

If a female employee is pregnant during her course of employment or can anticipate a pregnancy during her employment, there are certain rights guaranteed to her under the Pregnancy Discrimination Act which became effective April 20, 1979. The Act was passed by Congress in reaction to a Supreme Court decision which held that classifications based on pregnancy were *not* gender-based classifications and did not have a disparate impact on women. A second case decided by the Supreme Court held that since pregnancy classifications were not gender-based, then benefits for pregnancy were not required under Title VII. The result of these two decisions was that cases claiming discrimination because of pregnancy, either in terms of employment or benefits, could not be maintained under Title VII. The Pregnancy Discrimination Act was passed by Congress as an amendment to Title VII so that the intent of Congress would be clear both to the courts and to employers.

The Supreme Court, in both cases mentioned above, had indicated that Congressional intent to protect pregnancy and related problems was not clear under Title VII. Congress made its intentions quite clear when it stated the purpose of the Act to be ". . . that women affected by pregnancy and related conditions must be treated the same as other applicants and employees on the basis of their ability or inability to work." The Act specifically provides that if any written or unwritten employment practices exclude from employment opportunities or employment any women because of pregnancy, childbirth or related medical conditions, such policies will constitute a *prima facie* violation of Title VII.

The Act requires that every employer must consider each pregnant worker as an individual in determining her ability to continue with her employment or to be hired. Prior to the Act, employers were free to make employment decisions based on group stereotypes concerning the abilities/inabilities of pregnant women. Second, the employer must uniformly apply the same policies regarding sick leave, hospitalization coverage, disability insurance, seniority rights, accrual of vacation time and pay increases to the pregnant worker as it would apply those policies to a temporarily disabled male.

Perhaps the most significant aspect of the Pregnancy Discrimination Act is that Congress explicitly recognizes pregnancy as only a temporary disability. Prior to the passage of the Act, employers, with the approval of the United States Supreme Court, were able to enforce arbitrary and discriminatory practices against pregnant employees without fear of Title VII sanctions.

The granting of maternity leave has carried the greatest abuse in employment situations. Employers in the educational field were notorious for implementing leave policies that had arbitrary cut-off dates for beginning a maternity leave and date for resuming duties after childbirth. An example would be a policy requiring that all pregnant employees cease employment activities at the end of the 5th month of pregnancy, regardless of the individual employee's ability to carry on. Similarly, many employers instituted policies proscribing that a female employee could not return to work until three months after childbirth.

Today, these policies are in violation of Title VII, as amended by the Pregnancy Discrimination Act. A determination for continuing or resuming employment must be made as to each individual and her ability to perform her job. The ability to continue or resume employment activity can be determined by a physician's statement, by discussions between the employer and employee, and by a review of the employee's job.

The amount of time an employer must give for maternity leave is a question that can only be answered on a case by case basis. If there is an express maternity leave policy, that policy must grant the same privileges granted for leave due to any other temporary medical disability or condition. If there is no written medical leave policy, but the employer makes it a practice to grant such leaves, maternity leave time must be comparable. The same type of analysis applies when determining whether or not the employee is entitled to compensation during any leave period. That is, if the employer continues to pay male employees absent from work due to a temporary disability or illness for any specified period of time, then the employer must also continue to pay the female employee while on a maternity leave. If the employer does not have a written policy regarding payment of wages/salaries during leave time, the female employee on maternity leave must be granted the same type of compensation as the employer makes it a practice to pay to temporarily disabled male employees.

If, during the course of her pregnancy, an employee is required to take a leave because of medical complications (e.g., threatened miscarriage) but later recovers before childbirth, the employer cannot refuse to allow the employee to return to work. The employer can require verification from the woman's doctor that the complications which lead to the leave are no longer present and that the woman is able to return to work, but it may not impose arbitrary policies on a pregnant employee if those same policies are not imposed on temporarily disabled men.

Similarly, if an employee is unable to perform her normal job duties because of the pregnancy (e.g. chemistry teacher unable to work around chemicals) the employer must provide alternative duties, IF it provides the same flexibility for male employees working under a temporary disability. If the male chemistry teacher is unable to teach his classes because of medication he must take and the employer finds another spot for him, or arranges for a substitute, the employer must provide the same benefit for the pregnant employee.

Inevitably, a pregnant employee will need to take some time off during her pregnancy, at least for childbirth. The question then becomes: Will the job still be there after recovery from childbirth? The employer must hold open the job unless (1) the employee indicates she will not be returning, or (2) it does not hold open jobs for male employees recovering from a medical disability.

A dilemma arises for the pregnant worker where her employer has no written policy and hasn't established any unwritten practice regarding temporary medical disabilities.

The EEOC, in its guidelines, has indicated that the termination of a pregnant employee, where there is insufficient or no leave available for pregnancy and/or childbirth, violates the Act IF it has a disparate impact on employees of one sex. If an employee finds herself with a no-policy employer, the same type of analysis explained in Chapter II regarding disparate impact would be used.

Even though the Pregnancy Discrimination Act is very explicit regarding maternity leaves, an employer may be able to circumvent the Act if it can show that the arbitrary, discriminatory policy or lack of leave policy is based on a "bona fide" business necessity. In one case, the court upheld the discharge of a non-tenured teacher because she would be absent for part of the subsequent teaching year. The discharge was based on the school system's desire to minimize teacher absences REGARDLESS OF THE CAUSE. However, a number of factors need to be weighed in determining whether or not the policy is based on a bona fide business necessity. Some considerations to be taken into account would include the length of the absence, the availability of a qualified substitute during the leave, and the uniformity of application of the policy regarding leave. If the same policy does not apply to a male employee, the employer is going to be hard-pressed to prove business necessity regarding a female employee.

The right of a female employee to continue to accrue or receive benefits during a pregnancy-related disability is also provided for under the Act. Health insurance coverage for pregnancy and related problems must be provided to female employees on the same basis as other types of insured illnesses and disabilities. If the employer offers or provides any type of health care benefits, it may not exclude pregnancy coverage. This holds true regardless of the additional cost which may result from an increase in benefits. The only exception is that the employer need not provide coverage for abortions. However, insurance coverage must be available to cover expenses incurred for an abortion where the mother's life is in danger or where complications result from having had an abortion.

An employer may not charge an additional or increased deductible for claims arising because of pregnancy. The deductible must be the same as that provided for other claims of a similar nature. Additionally, the policy may not have any specified dollar amount ceiling if other covered disabilities or illnesses are not treated in the same manner.

Disability insurance, like health insurance, must be provided equally to male and female employees. Employers are beginning to include disability insurance in benefit packages offered to employees in order to defray the cost of temporary disabilities and to relieve the employer from paying wages during a disability. Title VII, as amended by the Pregnancy Discrimination Act, specifically requires that disability insurance be granted in a nondiscriminatory fashion. Benefits such as income maintenance can no longer be denied to pregnant employees if those benefits are offered to other employees suffering from a temporary medical disability.

The disability insurance offered may not provide for lower payments for pregnancy disabilities if all other medical disabilities are treated equally. If a male employee is entitled to receive a certain sum of money for so many weeks when recovering from surgery or a serious illness, those same benefits must be available to the female employee during a pregnancy disability or a disability related to a pregnancy.

The same principles as applied to health and disability insurance apply to seniority rights, accrual of vacation time and right to pay increases during a disability. An employer's policy concerning the accrual and crediting of seniority, vacation time and pay raises must be the same for employees absent from employment for pregnancy-related reasons as for those absent due to other medical problems.

The effect of the Act is simply to insure that women affected by pregnancy be treated the same as any other applicant or employee on the basis of their ability or inability to work. The overriding theme of the Act is EQUALITY— no preferential treatment or better benefits because of sex.

Related to disability because of pregnancy is the issue of the rights of women who have children to raise. The Pregnancy Discrimination Act does not specifically address the problems of employment and childrearing, but the EEOC Guidelines indicate that if an employer grants leaves of absence for non-employment reasons, it cannot deny a female employee the right to take a leave for childrearing purposes. If the employer allows time away for travel, for example, the female employee must be allowed time away from work to tend to her family responsibilities. It is very important for the female employee to know the employer's policy regarding non-employment and non-medical leave policies. If there are certain in-house procedures that must be followed, the employee will be required to follow them before filing any charge of discrimination with the EEOC.

The right to have time away from work for childrearing purposes has not been tested too extensively in the courts, but one decision has held that a mother could not be denied a leave of absence when the purpose of the leave was to continue breast-feeding her child so as to postpone the development of allergies in the child. The employer in that case did have a policy of allowing non-employment related leaves and the court felt that the female employee's request for leave time was as proper a request for leave as was a male employee's request to take a sabbatical for travel purposes.

Sexual Harassment

The increasing number of women in the workforce has brought an increase in the types of problems a woman must face once she begins working. Among these problems is that of sexual harassment. The result of sexual harassment can be devastating to a woman, who often feels compelled either to complacently accept the harassment or to quit the job and hope that her next place of employment will be free from harassment of a sexual nature.

There is a third alternative available to a woman who feels she has been sexually harassed. That alternative is to file a charge under Title VII and thereby protect the right to be free of harassment on her job, at least in certain situations. First of all, the harassment must in actuality be of a sexual nature. Second, the harassment must not only be sexual in nature, but it must also be made a condition of employment. Third, the harassing employee must be one in a supervisory capacity. This does not mean that the harassing employee must be your direct supervisor; he can be any supervisor employed by the employer. However, the harassing supervisor must make the harassment or compliance with it a condition of your employment.

One of the most difficult problems the female employee faces is proving that harassment is in fact sexual. The term "sexual harassment" is not one which can be placed into a formula where A + B = Harassment. The courts and administrative agencies can only look to subjective criteria in determining what is or is not harassment. The courts and agencies will try to determine if the acts were really harassment or if they were simply harmless horseply, or behavior that, although callous and inconsiderate, was nothing more than a practical joke. In some cases, it has been held that such actions as touching of the female employee's breast, placing contraceptives in her purse, using vulgar or profane language in her presence, were not acts of sexual harassment. On the other hand, lewd suggestions implying the female employee will go far in the corporate ranks, or repeated demands for sexual favors, have been held to constitute sexual harassment. It is not an easy determination to make and the courts will generally use their own discretion in determining what is or is not sexual harassment.

Once it has been determined that the advances or demands or actions of the harassing employee are sexual in nature, it must be determined if they are being made as a CONDITION of continued employment, job status, evaluations, promotion or other aspects of career development. By restricting the type of harassment to that made a condition of employment, the court is attempting to restrict its authority to employment-related problems and not problems of a personal nature. This philosophy of limiting the court's jurisdiction to work-related problems and not personal problems is one of the greatest impediments to asserting a charge of sexual harassment.

Many women find that they are subjected to all types of harassment on the job, but if the harassing employees are not supervisors or if the harassment is not a condition of employment, they will find themselves without a remedy under Title VII. However, many states have begun to enact legislation to cover work situations not covered by Title VII and allow women to file charges of sexual harassment against coworkers and non-supervisory personnel. These state statutes vary greatly from state to state in the amount and depth of protection provided to a female employee, but they may be helpful if Title VII will not cover the situation at hand.

Procedurally, the few EEOC and court decisions have indicated that it is mandatory that the female employee report the incidents of sexual harassment to the employer *before* filing any formal charge. The reason behind this requirement is to allow the employer to receive notice of the problem and then to take steps to put a stop to the harassment. The methods the employer may use are left to its discretion, but whatever the means chosen, they must put an immediate stop to the harassment.

When reporting an incident of sexual harassment, the female employee must be certain that she is reporting the problem to a proper authority. If there is a union at her place of employment, the employee should first check with the union officials to see if there is a designated person within the organization who handles harassment complaints. If not, the employee should determine who in the employer's organization should be contacted. This may be the university president, school board president, or department head. In any event, the employee should report the problem of harassment to a proper official and if she is uncertain who that person is, she should report it to as many officials as she feels might be appropriate.

An employer may not fire a female employee because she has filed a complaint of sexual harassment. If the employee is fired, she should *immediately* file a complaint with the EEOC or her state deferral agency. It is not a requirement of employment under Title VII that a female employee learn how to "get along" when she is the victim of sexual harassment. If an employee is fired by her employer for filing a complaint of sexual harassment, the employer's action in firing her will weigh heavily against it in any court or administrative agency proceeding.

When faced with a sexual harassment problem, the employee would be wise to educate herself in regards to: (1) the grievance procedure of the employer, i.e., is there a review board, arbitrator, or employee representative designated to handle these types of complaints; (2) whether the particular state has passed any legislation which extends protection further than Title VII; (3) what the state EEOC deferral agency has done in similar cases; and (4) if there is no relief available at the state level, what is the regional EEOC stance in sexual harassment cases.

The decision of an employee to file a sexual harassment complaint is difficult to make. It is difficult because, unlike other areas protected by Title VII, sexual harassment charges involve more than clear-cut problems of discrimination such as those seen in unequal pay or benefit discrimination. A charge of sexual harassment is a charge that involves a direct attack on the supervisor's ability as a supervisor and make-up as a person. The charge will also involve a severe scrutiny of the harassed employee's behavior. Did she invite harassment of a sexual nature by her attitudes, did she lead the supervisor on in hopes of advancement, or is the charge of harassment merely a personal vendetta.

The employee should be aware of the fact that the employer, the administrative agency and the courts will look at the types of questions put forth above in making a determination. However, if the employee has been subjected to sexual harassment, she should not be discouraged in either filing a complaint or making the problem known to the employer. The problem of harassment will not lessen by accepting it; the problem will only worsen, and that alternative could be far more difficult to accept in the long-run than the temporary problems the employee may encounter in filing a charge.

Chapter IV

WHAT TO DO ABOUT DISCRIMINATION

When a woman believes that she is the victim of sex discrimination in her job, she is likely to feel frustrated and angry. The frustration and anger are even greater if she does not know what steps to take in seeking a solution. *Procedure* is a highly technical and sometimes confusing area of civil rights law. While the law was developed to protect the rights of individuals, the procedural rules for implementing that law can sometimes prove to be a major obstacle in a perfectly valid complaint.

An attorney or an EEOC representative are the best resources to use in making sure that all procedural requirements are met. However, if you cannot afford an attorney, or if there is not enough time left in which to speak to an employee of the EEOC, you may have to proceed on your own. Even if you do retain an attorney or get help from the EEOC, you should still know the basic procedural rules in order to safeguard your Title VII complaint.

In order to better explain the various steps, decisions, and problems involved in filing a sex discrimination complaint, a hypotehtical situation of a "typical" female employee is described below. Any similarities to any real individual are merely coincidental, but not unlikely.

B. Kay Smith is a 1970 graduate of Michigan State University, 1972 graduate of Stanford University's masters program in Early Childhood Development. She was employed by CLS University on September 1, 1973 at the entry level position of adjunct professor.

Ms. Smith's beginning salary is $13,500; she receives life insurance, medical benefits, retirement benefits and various other fringe benefits.

R. A. Bud is a 1970 graduate of Michigan State University, 1972 graduate of Stanford University's masters program in Early Childhood Development. He too is employed by the University as an adjunct professor. He began his employment on January 1, 1974.

Mr. Bud's beginning salary is $18,500; he receives life insurance, medical benefits, retirement benefits and various other fringe benefits, including a University car and University housing.

Ms. Smith and Mr. Bud are good friends and have known each other since their undergraduate days when Ms. Smith tutored Mr. Bud. Ms. Smith graduated in the top 10% of her class, while Mr. Bud was in the top 20%.

Both are employed in the School of Education, both teach classes involved with early childhood development. Both are well-liked by faculty and students alike.

On January 1, 1980, the Department Chairman informs Mr. Bud that he has been doing a splendid job and he will be promoted to associate professor and receive tenure in the near future.

Mr. Bud is delighted and immediately contacts Ms. Smith to congratulate her on her similar good fortune. Ms. Smith is quite surprised and tells Mr. Bud that she has not been informed of any promotions or possible tenure.

Ms. Smith approaches the Department Chairman and asks why she has not been advised of any promotion or possibility of tenure. The answer is simple, she is told: (1) Mr. Bud is more qualified, (2) Mr. Bud needs the increased salary at the higher level, (3) Ms. Smith is pregnant and (4) Only one promotion/tenure spot was opened.

One week later Mr. Bud is promoted and granted tenure. Ms. Smith is livid.

What should she do? Does she have any basis for a sex discrimination complaint? These questions can only be answered after going through some preliminary investigation.

Assessing the Employment Situation

The first step is to assess the total situation. This assessment should not stop with the immediate problem at hand; each and every facet of the employment situation should be reviewed. In her initial angry response, Ms. Smith could focus only on the unfair denial of promotion and tenure. In fact, she is also being denied equal pay, equal fringe benefits, and perhaps even more.

Since Ms. Smith and Mr. Bud are on friendly terms, she could begin by talking to him. This should not be approached in an accusatory way, rather as a simple investigation into all of the facts. A friendly approach will probably get Ms. Smith more information than an "I've been wronged and now they are going to pay" attitude.

When talking with Mr. Bud, Ms. Smith should try to find out everything she can about his job and benefits. This includes salaries, fringe benefits, class load, job evaluations, student evaluations, etc. Every detail, even though it may seem trivial at the time, should be carefully examined. For instance, Ms. Smith may mention in passing that her health insurance policy really looked good until she discovered it didn't cover pregnancy. She may find out that Mr. Bud's wife is covered under his health insurance policy, including any pregnancy-related expenses.

If Ms. Smith is unable to find a male employee within her department who is willing to talk openly about the pay he receives and the benefits connected with his job, she could try to get the information from the school. She can request copies of all benefit packages given to male employees, a breakdown of salaries between males and females within her department, and any other pertinent information, including promotion and tenure policies. Trying to collect information from the school itself may prove time-consuming and frustrating. It is highly unlikely that any educational employer is going to willingly and quickly produce all of the information requested; but under the Freedom of Information Act she would be able to obtain enough information to make some general assessments and initial decisions.

After exploring all of the various policies, practices and employee benefits offered by the employer, Ms. Smith must then decide whether or not she is being discriminated against. Is she? Absolutely. There are several grounds, including unequal compensation, fringe benefits, promotion and tenure.

Now that Ms. Smith knows that she is being discriminated against, what does she do about it? Naturally she will want to consider the quickest, easiest, and least expensive way of asserting her equal employment rights. Therefore, the next thing she should investigate is whether or not her employer has any internal grievance procedures available for resolution of discrimination problems.

With the increasing awareness of educational employers as to their responsibilities to employees, and with the increasing numbers of cases being settled in favor of female employees, many institutions have developed internal guidelines and procedures to provide a quick and fair resolution to discrimination problems. A word of warning, however: internal grievance procedures have no legal status as far as Title VII is concerned. Any action taken by the university or employer on their own initiative is not binding on the EEOC or other agencies in applying the law. Many women who have relied solely on internal procedures have lost an otherwise valid Title VII claim because, while awaiting the outcome, they failed to meet the time requirements for filing under Title VII.

If Ms. Smith, for example, feels she might get an adequate remedy by pursuing internal relief, then she should try to do so. However, she should keep her other options open. This means that even though she has begun with internal proceedings, she must understand the Title VII filing procedures and deadlines and be prepared to file an action with the appropriate agency if there is no final resolution as those deadlines approach.

Consulting an Attorney

Also at this stage, Ms. Smith should consider consulting an attorney. It is not required that she retain an attorney for filing a sex discrimination charge under Title VII; but, depending on the complexity of the case, it may prove to be desirable. In any case, an initial consultation can greatly assist Ms. Smith in understanding the legal merits and problems involved in her particular case.

Most attorneys today will meet with you to simply sit down and discuss a problem, without any expectation that they be retained as attorney of record. Usually there will be a simple, flat rate charged for this meeting, which you can usually find out by calling the office.

There are several advantages to having a conference of this type. First, Ms. Smith is making contact with an attorney and finding out if she is comfortable with that person. Good rapport is an important aspect of the attorney-client relationship, and Ms. Smith will need to feel she can be totally honest with the attorney and have confidence in the attorney's ability to assist her. Second, Ms. Smith will get some basic legal advice before trying to solve her problem entirely on her own. Third, in the event that Ms. Smith later decides she needs to retain an attorney, she will already have laid the groundwork for her case. Talking to an attorney might also open up some new ideas which she may not have thought of, or did not know how to approach.

There are a number of ways to go about choosing an attorney. One of the best is by word-of-mouth. If Ms. Smith knew of any women who had filed sex discrimination complaints against an employer, she could contact these women to see if they had used an attorney and find out how they felt about that person. Generally, people who win their case are happy with the attorney and people who lose blame it on the ineptness of the attorney. So Ms. Smith should get beyond the win/loss record of the attorney and find out what the case involved. If Ms. Smith is unable to locate an attorney who specifically handles sex discrimination matters, she may begin her search by trying to find a firm or individual her friends have confidence in. Attorneys today are well aware of the limitations they must impose upon themselves as to their abilities and qualifications in handling certain matters. The practice of law is becoming highly specialized and any attorney who respects both the law and the potential client will be honest as to his/her abilities. The usual practice of attorneys is to refer cases to other attorneys who are more qualified, if they feel the matter is too far outside their area of interest or specialization.

Many state, local, or county bar associations maintain a lawyer referral service. These agencies can be very helpful if they classify attorneys by areas of expertise and interest. When contacting a referral service, ask for the name of an attorney who handles civil rights cases, employment discrimination matters, or women's rights issues. These three areas are all very closely related, and expertise in one generally means an understanding in others.

Some of the specific questions Ms. Smith might have about a prospective attorney are: number of years in private practice, prior administrative agency experience (many attorneys in private practice have worked for EEOC, or similar agencies), interest or expertise in employment discrimination cases, reputation in the community, ability to communicate, and demeanor. In addition, Ms. Smith should discuss fees with the attorney *prior* to any decision about retaining that individual. Before any work is actually undertaken by the attorney, the two parties should enter into a written retainer fee agreement.

The one absolute qualification an attorney must possess is a belief that she has a valid complaint of sex discrimination and a willingness to do everything within his/her power to protect Ms. Smith's employment rights. Without this belief, the attorney will prove highly ineffective. This basic quality can only be determined by personal contact and by discussion of the particular case and of the general problem of sex discrimination in employment.

At this point, Ms. Smith should have completed the following:

- talked to fellow employees;
- reviewed her employment contract, benefit package, and other terms of employment, and compared them with those of her fellow employees;
- investigated her employer's internal procedures, if any, for complaints involving discriminatory employment practices;
- consulted an attorney, if desired, to discuss the merits of her case.

It is apparent after the investigation is finished that Ms. Smith has indeed been discriminated against. The discriminatory acts include the following:

1. Unequal pay scales for male and female employees
2. Discriminatory health insurance coverage
3. Fringe benefit inequities
4. Denial of tenure on the basis of sex
5. Denial of promotion on the basis of sex
6. Denial of promotion and tenure because of her pregnancy.

The problem situation of Ms. Smith is not atypical. The average sex discrimination in employment complaint will involve more than one simple issue. This is why it is so important to carefully review and assess the entire employment environment. All six of the above discriminatory acts can be resolved by filing one complaint under Title VII.

Building a Case

With the issues so clearly drawn in the investigatory stage, Ms. Smith must now determine what it is she needs to prove for each issue.

The general rule for proving a discrimination charge is that the employee must show that she was subjected to some adverse employment action, and that others of similar qualifications and in similar circumstances but of a different sex were not subjected to the same adverse action. *McDonnell Douglas Corp. v.* Green, 411 U.S. 792 (1973). This rule simply means that in proving a charge of sex discrimination in employment a woman is going to have to present a COMPARABLE MALE.

When producing her comparable male, a woman must try to find a male employee as closely similar to her as possible. This means a man who has been employed the same or similar length of time, with similar qualifications (degrees, prior experience) similar responsibilities, and the same or very similar job classification. In our example, Mr. Bud is the comparable male. This is the ideal situation in which there is someone so closely similar it would be impossible to claim that they are not comparable.

In actuality, a comparable male is sometimes more difficult to prove. The male employee must be real, he must exist, and there must be a basis upon which to compare the two employees and show the disparity in employment opportunities and benefits.

If there is a problem in showing one male to be in the similar employment situation to that of the female, it will be necessary to create a wider comparison. For instance, the woman could obtain salary, ranking and tenure status for all the male employees within her department. At the same time, she would prepare a composite picture of the same data for the women in the department. By preparing this department analysis, she may be able to show a pattern or practice of discrimination against all women within that particular department.

The biggest drawback to this type of analysis may be the number of women employed within the involved department. For instance, on the elementary school level, if a qualified woman is denied promotion to vice-principal in a school in which she is one of only four female teachers out of 35 teachers, there may be insufficient grounds for creating a comparison. There may be enough difference between the men and women employees so that the school board could argue that the decision of whom to promote was not made on the basis of sex, but rather, sheer seniority, qualification, etc. However, the female teacher should not be discouraged.

She should proceed to prepare a system-wide analysis of the employment situations of all the men and women within the school system. The data should be broken down on the basis of sex, length of employment, educational background, prior teaching experience, and salary. By creating a comprehensive picture, she may be able to show an on-going discriminatory practice by the school board or administrators.

The most desirable and effective way to prove a claim of sex discrimination in employment is to show a comparable male and also show how he is given greater opportunity and/or benefit than the female counterpart. System-wide or department-wide analysis should only be used as a last resort, or when there is a need to show a continuation of past discriminatory practices. These larger, more comprehensive pictures, will be most useful when a complaint involves matters such as denial of maternity leave, fringe benefit inequities, overcontributions to retirement programs, and problems involving matters which have been clearly and explicitly regulated by Title VII.

The more personal in nature the claim is, the narrower the comparison of employees should be. Personal type claims involve pay, promotion and tenure. These areas all involve highly specific and subjective factors, which must be shown on a person by person basis. But this is not to say that in cases where it is impossible to create a single comparable male, a larger grouping of employees should not be used for comparison purposes.

Another way to prove discrimination is to show that a male with *less* qualifications, responsibilities, length of employment, etc. is receiving GREATER benefits and employment opportunities than a woman with better qualifications. Although the two employees are not closely similar, it will be difficult for an employer to explain away the apparent differences between the pay, benefits or status of the two employees.

Filing a Complaint

Now that Ms. Smith knows upon what grounds she is going to base her sex discrimination complaint and how to go about proving it, she must decide on the best strategy for asserting her equal employment rights. There are four possible alternatives: (1) internal grievance—if a system exists, (2) state action, (3) federal action, and (4) court action.

Internal Grievance Procedures

The great advantage of internal grievance procedures is that they are usually faster, more efficient and more amicable. Internal procedures are completely governed by the involved institution, with a set of rules, regulations and procedures established by the school board, grievance committee, or department heads. If Ms. Smith decides to seek remedy through internal procedures, she will have to become familiar with the specific procedural requirements of her university.

Again, she must remember that filing a complaint through internal procedures does not satisfy any *legal* requirements under Title VII or under state fair employment law, nor does any internal action affect any legal right of action she may possess under the various laws. Ms. Smith may ultimately need to utilize state or federal laws to resolve her sex discrimination problems. In order to protect her right to do so, she may have to file a complaint with the appropriate state or federal agency while her internal complaint is still pending. This will insure that she has met the time requirements for filing a legal complaint should that become necessary.

If no internal procedures exist, or if internal action does not result in a satisfactory result, the woman employee must pursue her claim under the various laws designed to protect her rights. In addition to federal laws which pertain to equal employment rights, many of the states have passed Fair Employment Practice laws or Civil Rights laws. In these states, federal and state governments have "concurrent jurisdiction" over sex discrimination in employment. Which law should a woman file under—state or federal? What agency should she file with? To avoid any confusion, Title VII has set up very explicit, detailed procedures to be followed in those states which have employment laws as comprehensive as the federal law.

State Action

Title VII has created state agencies known as 706 Deferral Agencies in those states which have an adequate anti-discrimination statute and enforcement agency. In any state designated as a 706 Agency state, the EEOC automatically defers jurisdiction to the state agency, giving the state first chance at solving the sex discrimination complaint *using state law.*

Ms. Smith resides in a state with 706 Deferral status. This means that she must *first* file her sex discrimination complaint with the state agency, and that she must abide by the procedural requirements and substantive law of her state.

For the most part, state and federal laws and procedural requirements are very similar. However, there is one very crucial way in which they differ — the time limits within which a sex discrimination complaint must be filed. According to federal law, a woman has 180 days from the date of the occurrence of a discriminatory act in which to file her complaint of sex discrimination, but at the state level this time period can be anywhere from 60 days to 360 days from the date of occurrence.

Appendix A sets out the name and address of the agency in each state with 706 Deferral status. Ms. Smith should immediately contact her state agency to determine exactly what her state requires insofar as time limits are concerned. The majority of civil rights agencies, fair employment law agencies, etc., are staffed with personnel trained to answer all questions regarding procedural technicalities, and they will be able to answer any question she may have. If the agency personnel does not appear to know the answer to her question, she can simply go to the statute and learn what particular requirements her state imposes upon an employee. Again, the vast majority of 706 agencies will keep on hand copies of the laws under which sex discrimination complaints can be filed.

Once a complaint is filed with the 706 Deferral Agency, the state has 60 days (120 days if it is the agency's first year of operation) in which to resolve the complaint. After 60 days have passed and before the 180-day federal deadline has passed, if the state agency hasn't satisfactorily resolved the matter, the complainant-employee may request that the matter be transferred to the regional EEOC office for a final resolution using the federal law—Title VII.

Under Title VII the EEOC is *required* to assume jurisdiction of a matter if the 60 days for the 706 Agency's decision has passed *and* the EEOC has been notified that no
resolution has been made of the sex discrimination complaint. The statutory language appears to make the transfer
of the complaint the responsibility of the state agency; however, as a practical matter, the complaint will in all likelihood remain in a state agency unless the complainant requests that it be transferred.

If her case is still pending after 60 (120) days, Ms. Smith
is faced with another decision: Should she remain in her
state 706 agency, or should she have the matter transferred
to the regional EEOC office. The biggest factor to be considered is that of time. If the state agency has spent a great
deal of time investigating the complaint and is very close to
making a decision, than it would be best to stay in the jurisdiction of the state agency until that decision is made. On the
other hand, if the state 706 agency has been slow in handling
the matter, then it might be a good idea to transfer the complaint to the federal agency. If a file is transferred to the
EEOC, the EEOC will undertake to conduct its own investigation, which might include a repetition of the investigative
work already done by the state 706 agency.

There are several distinct advantages in transferring the
complaint to the federal offices. First, the federal agency
usually carries more clout, just because it is a federal agency.
All public schools and universities are dependent upon financial aid from the various governmental authorities, the greatest being the federal government. Second, the EEOC will

have at its easy disposal the various EEOC forms required to be filed by schools and universities and will be able to rely upon those forms in determining if the employer is carrying on a system-wide scheme of sex discrimination. Additionally, the fact that a female employee is so convinced of her rights under the law that she is willing to pursue them through all possible avenues of redress may cause the employer to take her claim more seriously.

In those states which do not have 706 Deferral Agencies, a woman files directly with her regional EEOC office (Appendix B) and follows the procedure set out under Title VII. The process and resolution of her case would be based on federal law from the beginning.

Federal Action

Title VII requires that a discrimination charge be made within 180 days of the occurrence of the discrimination. After a complaint is filed, the employer is notified by the agency, normally by mail within 10 days after receipt of the complaint. After the complaint is filed, the employer is known as the respondent.

After a charge has been filed with the EEOC and the parties have been notified, the EEOC will conduct an investigation. The purpose of the investigation is to determine whether "reasonable cause" exists to believe Title VII has been violated. Because of the great number of charges filed with it, the EEOC has developed the investigatory stage to weed out claims which, on their face, do not show a violation of Title VII.

Reasonable cause simply means that the EEOC will attempt to find out exactly what the charging party is complaining of and whether it is a violation of Title VII. In order to make this determination, the investigating official can ask the charging party for a detailed statement specifying the alleged unlawful act and the date it occurred, and the reason why the employee believes said acts or practices are discriminatory. A properly drawn complaint can help to speed this stage of the agency proceedings. The rules of procedure under Title VII call for a "clear and concise" statement of facts, but the more detailed in the original complaint, the less time spent in the investigation stage.

The investigating official may also require a fact-finding conference with the parties. This conference is informal and is intended to define the issues, determine which elements of the issues are undisputed, resolve those issues which can be resolved and determine if there is a basis for settlement.

If the official does make a determination that there is reasonable cause to believe Title VII has been violated, the matter will proceed; if reasonable cause is not found, the matter will be dismissed. The dismissal of a charge by the EEOC means the employee may either accept that decision or file a civil suit in court. The court will give great weight to the decisions of any administrative agency, but those decisions are not dispositive of the case. The decision to file a private civil action should be made only after consultation with an attorney and a thorough evaluation of the merits of the charge.

If reasonable cause is found, the next step is conference, conciliation and persuasion. This is simply the method by which the EEOC will try to reach a negotiated settlement between the parties. The ultimate goal of the EEOC is to reach an amicable settlement of the dispute and to avoid the cost of litigation. The type and terms of settlement are largely left to the charging party and the respondent. At this stage, the EEOC acts as an arbitrator, rather than a final decision maker. However, the EEOC does advise the parties of their rights under the law and makes decisions as to the validity of any claim. The employer and employee can each make offers of settlement, and the EEOC can issue opinions as to the offers.

If conferences, conciliation and persuasion do not resolve the dispute, a court action can be filed either by the EEOC or the charging party. The EEOC may file suit in federal court anytime after 30 days of filing the sex discrimination complaint if an agreement is not reached.

Court Action

If the charging party wishes to start an action in court on her own at this point, she can do so only upon the issuance of a right to sue letter by the EEOC to her. A right to sue letter is issued when the charging party requests, in writing, that the letter be issued. The EEOC must issue the letter if (a) 180 days have elapsed since filing the charge with the EEOC or (b) 180 days have not gone by, but it appears unlikely the administrative proceedings will not be finished within 180 days of the filing date.

Once the right to sue letter has been issued, all proceedings stop with the EEOC. However, the EEOC can continue to be of assistance to the charging party, if she so desires.

The employee must file an action in the proper court, within 90 days of receipt of the right to sue letter. The filing of a civil action should be done only after careful consideration of all the factors involved: what the cost will be, the merits of the case, how much weight will be given to any administrative agency decision, and the time involved.

The decision of the administrative agency will not be binding upon the court where a lawsuit is filed. However, the court will take into consideration the agency's expertise in the area of employment discrimination, the amount of investigation, etc. that went into the agency decision, and will accord the decision some weight in arriving at its own verdict.

Many sex discrimination complaints are ultimately resolved in court proceedings after progressing through state
and federal agencies. In addition, increasing numbers of women are choosing to initiate a charge of discrimination
through private civil court action from the beginning. The
reason for this is primarily that of time. With the great back-
log of cases in an administrative agency, many women feel
that they can achieve a quicker resolution of their problem
by filing a private civil lawsuit and completely bystepping
the agencies.

If Ms. Smith had decided that she wanted to pursue her
remedies in a court of law at the outset, she would have been
well advised to retain an attorney to represent her throughout the proceedings. To begin a court action, a complaint
has to be prepared and filed. This complaint, however, would
be far more complex and detailed than that which can be filed
with a 706 agency or the EEOC. When proceeding in an
agency—either state or federal—she would have the agency
personnel available to assist her in preparing and pursuing
her claim. When filing a civil lawsuit, she would be completely on her own. Being involved in a civil lawsuit carries with
it a variety of legal technicalities which have to be dealt
with throughout the duration of the lawsuit and the use of an
attorney would probably be essential in handling them.

If a woman is unable to retain an attorney and still desires to pursue her cause of action in a court of law, she
should discover whether there are any local groups which

have a commitment or interest in sex discrimination problems. Some of these groups are able to provide highly informed assistance with the legal technicalities of sex discrimination charges. However, an attorney would still be first choice.

When and How To File

The single most important aspect of filing a sex discrimination complaint is knowing WHEN to file it. As stated above, state and federal law differs as to when a complaint must be filed. Title VII requires that a discrimination charge be made within 180 days of the occurrence of a discriminatory act. On the state level, the only difference is the number of days in which to file, but the requirement that the complaint be filed within a certain number of days from the occurrence of a discriminatory act remains.

Referring back to Ms. Smith's case, we see that she has a number of different issues upon which to base her complaint, all of which happened at different times, and some which still continue to occur (i.e., lower rate of pay). Under the various laws—state and federal—one complaint may be filed which alleges all discriminatory acts. The question then becomes: Which discriminatory act is the measuring date for purposes of satisfying the complaint filing requirements?

In the example given, Ms. Smith's most recent discrimination occurred on the date of her last paycheck when she received a discriminatory wage. The cases involving unequal pay for equal employees will include an argument that the discriminatory act is an ongoing and continuous violation of the law and is, therefore, timely as of the date of filing the complaint.

In the situation of unequal fringe benefits, Ms. Smith could also use the date that she discovered the inequities as the time period in which the statutory time limit began to run.

As to the date to be considered in the discriminatory denial of tenure and promotion, a number of dates are involved. The date he was actually promoted and given tenure, the date Ms. Smith requested she be given tenure and a promotion, and the date she was denied her request. As a general rule in cases such as this one where a variety of dates are involved, it is best to use the date of some *official* action by the employer. That is, the date Mr. Bud's promotion/tenure became effective or the date Ms. Smith was officially denied promotion/tenure.

The general rule is that the most recent date of a discriminatory act will be used to determine if the complaint was filed within the time period required by law. As the above example indicates, the more discriminatory acts involved, the greater the number of different dates, and the greater the chance for confusion as to which date will serve as the measuring date. Therefore, a woman who believes she has been discriminated against should file her complaint as soon after the discriminatory act as possible. The time limits set by statute are usually strictly enforced, so the longer the delay in filing a sex discrimination complaint, the greater the chance the complaint will be untimely filed.

The actual form of a sex discrimination charge is simple. It must be in writing and verified. Verified means that the person signing the complaint must do so under oath before a notary public, an authorized representative of the EEOC or any other person authorized to administer oaths. A charge of discrimination can be brought either by the employee herself, or it can be filed on her behalf. After the complaint is filed, the employee is referred to as the charging party.

The complaint, or charge, must contain the following:

1. Full name, address and telephone number of the charging party;
2. Full name and address of the person against whom the charge is made;
3. A clear and concise statement of the facts, including pertinent dates, constituting the alleged unlawful employment practices;
4. If known, the approximate number of employees of the employer;
5. A statement whether any proceedings involving the alleged unlawful employment practices have been commenced before a state or local agency, and if so, the date said action began and the name of the agency.

The EEOC guidelines require a clear and concise statement of facts. This requirement is the foundation of any charge. It is absolutely essential that the charging party allege an unlawful discriminatory act. It is not sufficient to simply allege that a female employee is not treated fairly by the employer. Specific discriminatory acts must be contained in the charge. In Ms. Smith's case, the medical benefit plan treats men differently from women. In her complaint, she must say how it treats them differently, i.e., the wives of male employees are provided pregnancy coverage under the health insurance policy and female employees are not. For each of the issues involved, Ms. Smith will have to say what the problem is and why it is a problem.

For example, she is being paid less than Mr. Bud. Ms. Smith must allege the fact that she is being paid less, and further that she is being paid less than her comparable male, Mr. Bud. Some problems will involve a system-wide allegation, such as a discriminatory practice or pattern in the promotion of female employees. Ms. Smith would have to allege that in fact the discrimination existed on a system-wide basis and she would have to be prepared to later introduce her proofs supporting the allegations.

The basic rule is that when a party alleges something, she must be able to support that allegation at a later date with adequate and sufficient proofs. The charging party should include all of the discriminatory acts or practices she feels the employer has committed when filing her original charge. However, any and all alleged offenses must be supportable and made in good faith.

The number of sex discrimination complaints and court actions is increasing rapidly. In addition, more and more complaints and law suits are being settled, both in and out of court, in favor of women. However, any woman who files a sex discrimination complaint should be aware of some rather harsh realities.

First, it is unlikely that there will be any expedient, overnight resolution of the issue. The state and federal agencies that she will have to deal with are deluged with discrimination complaints, and although the law encourages and promotes quick resolutions, the reality of the situation is that there are far more complaints being filed than available personnel.

A charge of sex discrimination against one's employer entails some very real human costs in addition to the obvious financial and time investments. The process may well generate antagonism and hostility, and there may at times be heavy emotional, mental and physical strains upon a woman who asserts her legally guaranteed rights. In a sex discrimination complaint, as in any other charge wherein wrongdoing is alleged, the individual accused of wrongdoing will defend his innocence to the very end. It would be unusual indeed to have an employer simply agree that he was in fact discriminating against an employee on the basis of sex.

On the other hand, there is much to be gained, both for the individual in terms of specific remedies, and for all women in the attainment of equal employment opportunity. Only if women are willing to assert their equal employment rights will the laws have any real weight, force, or effect.

THE APPENDICES

The information contained in the following appendices was obtained from the Equal Employment Opportunity Commission, Washington, D.C.

Appendix A is a state-by-state listing of the 706 deferral agencies within that state. Most states have only one agency indicated, while others reflect a number of different agencies. In those states having more than one deferral agency a woman should contact the one nearest to her and inquire as to whether or not that is the proper agency for her complaint to be filed with.

Six of the states, Alabama, Arkansas, Louisiana, Mississippi, North Carolina and North Dakota, do not have 706 agencies, and a woman who resides in one of these states should look up her individual state listing to find out which EEOC District her state is in.

Appendix B is a listing of the EEOC District Offices. A few of the districts handle only one state, while other district offices are responsible for a number of states which are within their district. For example, the Denver Office receives complaints from Colorado, Montana, Nebraska, North Dakota, South Dakota and Wyoming. This does not mean that a woman in Wyoming is going to have to travel to Denver for any administrative hearings, however. The District Office serves as the central receiving area for all Title VII complaints and will distribute the complaints to the appropriate EEOC office closest to the complainant. If a woman resides in an EEOC district which is responsible for a number of states, she should contact the EEOC office and find out for certain where her complaint should be filed for quickest processing.

APPENDIX A

STATE	AGENCY ADDRESS	EEOC REGION
Alabama	None	Atlanta
Alaska	Human Rights Commission 204 East 5th Ave., Rom 213 Anchorage, Alaska 99501 907 — 276-7414	Seattle
Arkansas	None	Dallas
Arizona	Civil Rights Division 1645, West Jefferson St. Phoenix, Arizona 85007	Phoenix
California	Fair Employment Practices Commission P.O. Box 603 San Francisco, CA 94101 (415) 557-2000	San Francisco
Connecticut	Commission on Human Rights & Opportunities 90 Washington Street Hartford, Connecticut 06115 (203) 566-4895	New York
Colorado	Civil Rights Commission 1525 Sherman Street, Room 600C Denver, Colorado 80203 (303) 839-2621	Denver
Delaware	Anti-Discrimination Section 820 North French St., 6th Floor State Office Bldg. Wilmington, Delaware 19801 (302) 517-2900	Philadelphia

State	Agency Address	EEOC Region
District of Columbia	Office of Human Rights Lansburgh Bldg. 400 8th St., NW Room 104 Washington DC 20001 (202) 727-6523	Baltimore
Florida	Dade County Fair Housing and Employment Appeals Board 1515 N.W. 7th St., Room 109 Miami, Florida 33125 (305) 547-7840	Miami
	Florida Commission on Human Relations Montgomery Bldg., Suite 100 2562 Executive Ctr. Circle, East Tallahassee, Florida 32301 (904) 488-7082	
	Jacksonville Community Relations Commission Courthouse, Room 406 Jacksonville, Florida 32202 (904) 633-2010	
	Orlando Human Relations Commission 400 South Orange Ave., Suite 103 Orlando, Florida 32801 (305) 849-2122	

State	Agency Address	EEOC Region
Georgia	Augusta-Richmond County Human Relations Commission 500 Building, Suite 400 Augusta, Georgia 30902 (404) 724-2246	Atlanta
	Office of Fair Employment Practices 254 Washington St., SW, Suite 685 Atlanta, Georgia 30334 (404) 656-1736	
Hawaii	Department of Labor & Industrial Relations-Enforcement Division 888 Mililani St., Room 401 Honolulu, Hawaii 96813 (808) 548-3150	San Francisco
Idaho	Human Rights Commission Statehouse Boise, Idaho 83720 (208) 384-2873	Seattle
Illinois	Fair Employment Practices Commission 179 West Washington St., 6th Fl. Chicago, Illinois 60602 (312) 793-6200	Chicago

State	Agency Address	EEOC Region
Indiana	East Chicago Human Rights Commission City Hall, Room 9 4525 Indianapolis Blvd. East Chicago, IN 46312 (219) 392-8236	Indianapolis
	Fort Wayne Human Relations Commission One Main St., Room 680 Fort Wayne, IN 46802 (219) 423-7664	
	Gary Human Relations Commission 401 Broadway Gary, IN 46404 (219) 944-6541	
	Civil Rights Commission 311 West Washington Indianapolis, IN 46204 (317) 633-5072	
	South Bend Human Rights Commission 227 W. Jefferson Blvd. South Bend, IN 46601 (219) 284-9355	

State	Agency Address	EEOC Region
Iowa	Civil Rights Commission 507 Tenth St., 8th Floor Des Moines, Iowa 50319 (515) 281-4121	Milwaukee
Kansas	Commission on Civil Rights 535 Kansas Ave., 5th Floor Topeka, Kansas 66603 (913) 296-3206	St. Louis
Kentucky	Lexington-Fayette Human Rights Commission 207 North Upper Street Lexington, KY 40507 (606) 252-4931	Memphis
Louisiana	None	Dallas
Maine	Human Rights Commission Statehouse Augusta, Maine 04330 (207) 289-2326	New York
Maryland	Baltimore Community Relations Commission 100 North Eutaw St. Baltimore, Maryland 21201 (301) 396-3141 Howard County Human Rights Commission John Lee Carroll Bldg. 3450 Courthouse Drive Ellicott City, Maryland 21043 (301) 992-2162	Baltimore

State	Agency Address	EEOC Region
	Commission on Human Relations Baltimore Metro Plaza, Mondawmin Mall Suite 300 Baltimore, Maryland 21215 (301) 383-7600	
	Montgomery County Human Relations Commission 6400 Democracy Blvd. Bethesda, Maryland 20034 (301) 468-4260	
Massachusetts	Commission Against Discrimination One Ashburton Place Boston, Massachusetts 02108 (617) 727-7319	
Michigan	Department of Civil Rights Michigan Plaza Bldg. 1200 Sixth Avenue Detroit, MI 48226 (313) 256-2580	Detroit
Minnesota	Minneapolis Department of Civil Rights 2649 Park Ave., South Minneapolis, Minnesota 55101 (612) 348-7736	Milwaukee
	Department of Human Rights 240 Bremer Building 7th & Robert Street St. Paul, Minnesota 55101 (612) 296-5665	
Mississippi	None	Atlanta

State	Agency Address	EEOC Region
Missouri	Commission on Human Rights P.O. Box 1129 Jefferson City, Missouri 65101 (314) 751-3325	St. Louis
	St. Louis Civil Rights Enforcement Agency 3rd Floor, Civil Courts Bldg. St. Louis, Missouri 63101 (314) 622-3301	
Montana	Human Rights Division 616 Helena Ave., Steamboat Block—Suite 300 Helena, Montana 59601	Denver
Nebraska	Equal Opportunity Commission 301 Centennial Mall South 5th Floor Lincoln, Nebraska 68509	
	Omaha Human Rights Dept. 1819 Farnam St., Suite 502 Omaha, Nebraska 68102 (402) 444-5050	Denver
Nevada	Commission on Equal Rights of Citizens 1515 E. Tropicana, Suite 590 Las Vegas, Nevada 89158 (702) 386-5304	Los Angeles, California
New Hampshire	State Commission for Human Rights 61 South Spring St. Concord, New Hampshire 03301 (603) 271-2767	New York

State	Agency Address	EEOC Region
New Jersey	Division on Civil Rights 1110 Raymond Blvd. Newark, New Jersey 07102 (201) 648-2700	Philadelphia
New Mexico	Human Rights Commission 303 Bataan Memorial Bldg. Santa Fe, New Mexico 87503 (505) 827-5681	Phoenix
New York	New York City Commission on Human Rights 52 Duane Street New York, New York 10007 (212) 566-5588 New York State Division of Human Rights 2 World Trade Center New York, New York 10047 (212) 488-2940	New York
North Carolina	None	Atlanta
North Dakota	Dept. of Labor	Denver
Ohio	Civil Rights Commission 220 Parsons Avenue Columbus, Ohio 43215 (614) 466-5133	Cleveland
Oklahoma	Human Rights Commission P.O. Box 52945 Oklahoma City, Oklahoma 73152 (405) 521-3442	Dallas

State	Agency Address	EEOC Region
Oregon	Bureau of Labor Civil Rights Division 1400 S.W. 5th Avenue Portland, Oregon 97201 (503) 229-6076	Seattle
Pennsylvania	Human Rights Commission 100 N. Cameron Street P.O. Box 3145 Harrisburgh, Pennsylvania 17101 (717) 787-4410	
	Philadelphia Commission on Human Relations 601 City Hall Annex Philadelphia, Penn. 19107 (215) 686-4673 Pittsburgh Commission on Human Relations 908 City-County Bldg. Pittsburgh, Pa. 15219 (412) 255-2600	Philadelphia
Rhode Island	Commission for Human Rights 334 Westminister Mall Providence, Rhode Island 02903 (401) 277-2661	New York
South Carolina	Human Affairs Commission P.O. Box 11300 Columbia, South Carolina 29211 (803) 758-2748	Atlanta

State	Agency Address	EEOC Region
South Dakota	Division of Human Rights State Capitol Pierre, SD 57501 (605) 773-4183	Denver
Tennessee	Commission for Human Development 208 Tennessee Building 535 Church Street Nashville, Tennessee 37219 (615) 741-5825	Memphis
Texas	Fort Worth Human Relations Commission 1000 Throckmorton St. Ft. Worth, Texas 76102 (817) 870-6000	Dallas
	Austin Human Relations Commission P.O. Box 1088 Austin, TX 78767 (512) 472-9168	
	Corpus Christi Human Relations Commission 101 N. Shoreline Corpus Christi, Texas 78408 (512) 884-3011	Houston
Utah	Anti-Discrimination Division 350 East 500 South Salt Lake City, Utah 84111 (801) 533-5552	Phoenix

State	Agency Address	EEOC Region
Vermont	Attorney General's Office 109 State Street Montpelier, Vermont 05602 (802) 828-3171	New York
Virginia	Alexandria Human Rights Commission P.O. Box 178 Alexandria, Virginia 22313	Baltimore
	Fairfax County Human Rights Commission Circle Towers Office Bldg. 9401 Lee Highway, Suite 206 Fairfax, Virginia 22030 (703) 691-2953	
Washington	Seattle Human Rights Dept. 105 14th Avenue, Suite C Seattle, Washington 98122 (206) 625-4381	Seattle
	Tacoma Human Relations Commission 740 St. Helens, Room 307 Tacoma, Washington 98402 (206) 593-4334	
	Washington State Human Rights Commission 1601 2nd Avenue Bldg. 4th Floor Seattle, Washington 98101 (206) 464-6500	
West Virginia	Human Rights Commission 215 Professional Building 1036 Quarrier Street Charleston, West Virginia 25301 (304) 348-2616	Philadelphia

State	Agency Address	EEOC Region
Wisconsin	Equal Rights Division Dept. of Industry, Labor & Human Relations 201 E. Washington Avenue Madison, Wisconsin 53702 (608) 266-0946	Milwaukee
Wyoming	Fair Employment Commission Barrett Building, 4th Floor Cheyenne, Wyoming 82002 (307) 777-7261	Denver
Puerto Rico	Anti-Discrimination Unit 414 Barbosa Avenue Hato Rey, Puerto Rico 00917 (809) 763-4022	New York
Virgin Islands	Department of Labor P.O. Box 148, Charlotte Amalie St. Thomas, Virgin Islands 00801 (809) 774-2967	New York

APPENDIX B

District EEOC Offices	States
Indianapolis District Office Federal Building, U.S. Courthouse 46 East Ohio Street, Room 456 Indianapolis, Indiana 46204	Indiana
Los Angeles District Office 3255 Wilshire Blvd., 9th Floor Los Angeles, California 90010	Nevada
Memphis District Office 1407 Union Ave., Suite 502 Memphis, Tennessee 38104	Kentucky, Tennessee
Miami District Office DuPont Plaza Center, Suite 414 300 Biscayne Blvd. Way Miami, Florida 33131	Florida
Milwaukee District Office 342 North Water Street, Room 612 Milwaukee, Wisconsin 53202	Iowa, Minnesota, Wisconsin
New York District Office 90 Church Street, Room 1301 New York, New York 10007	Connecticut, Maine, Massachusetts, New Hampshire, New York, Puerto Rico, Rhode Island, Vermont, Virgin Islands
Philadelphia District Office 127 North 4th Street, Suite 200 Philadelphia, Pennsylvania 19106	Delaware, New Jersey, Pennsylvania, West Virginia
Phoenix District Office 201 North Central Avenue, Suite 1450 Phoenix, Arizona 85073	Arizona, New Mexico, Utah

District EEOC Offices	States
San Francisco District Office 1390 Market St., Suite 325 San Francisco, California 94102	California, Hawaii
Seattle District Office Dexter Horton Building 710 Second Avenue Seattle, Washington 98104	Alaska, Idaho, Oregon, Washington
St. Louis District Office 1601 Olive Street St. Louis, Missouri 63103	Kansas, Missouri

Date Due